"This marvelously clear Introduction to Lacan is truly a pleasure to read, a deeply intelligent and concise guide to Lacan's famously complex theoretical edifice and its brilliant and fascinating logic. Beautifully written, sparklingly with insights, their text condenses an enormous body of work, leading us from the origins of Lacan's theory to its inspiring therapeutic culmination: the vision of a psychoanalysis that liberates desire and frees us from the twin dilemmas of submitting or resisting the desire of the other."

Jessica Benjamin

"This small book by Yadlin-Gadot and Hadar offers a big achievement. It is introductory in its lucidity and minimal use of jargon, but it is simultaneously subtly sophisticated and utterly non-trivial. It articulates a dimension of human existence relevant not only to the psychoanalytic field, across its various theories and methodologies, but also to any scholar of ideological struggles and of subjectivity as such. It brings out the genius of Lacan as an interpreter of Freud and a remarkably original thinker, whose ideas influenced Western culture as a whole."

Slavoj Zizek

"Lacanian Psychoanalysis is, worldwide, now one of the most important psychoanalytic approaches, yet it still often seems obscure and inaccessible. In this timely new introduction, Shlomit Yadlin-Gadot and Uri Hadar provide a remarkably clear account of Lacan's central concepts. They focus especially on the 'subject-other' relationship, showing how Lacan gives us tools to understand human psychological development in its social-political context, in so doing offering an indispensable guide to psychosocial life."

Professor Stephen Frosch, Department of Psychosocial Studies, Birkbeck, University of London, UK

"I have never read a book that presents Lacanian thought with such clarity and sharpness while moving lively and freely between Lacanian concepts and their contemporary, original interpretation. This is not only an outstanding textbook dealing with Lacanian thought but a simultaneously poetic and clear, playful and rigorous. This is an extraordinary achievement in any context, but it is especially praiseworthy when it comes to a book dealing with the complicated language of Lacan."

Dana Amir

Lacanian Psychoanalysis

Lacanian Psychoanalysis: A Contemporary Introduction sees Shlomit Yadlin-Gadot and Uri Hadar provide an original approach to the elaborate and complex world of Jacques Lacan, one of psychoanalysis's most innovative thinkers.

This succinct introductory volume offers a fresh exposition of Lacanian thought, marking the philosophic influences and sensibilities that shaped it, and presenting its ideas and concepts in a simple language. Illustrations that range from the clinical and cultural to daily contemporary experience enliven the theory and make it easily accessible. The Lacanian psyche is thoroughly explained and described, unfolding as a drama of desire and jouissance, of hopes and disillusions. Its elusive subject is predicated upon otherness and decentered by its various forms: language and culture, meaningful people and the body. From this perspective, the authors illustrate how Lacan showed that love, sex, politics and therapy always involve the desire to be with the other but, at the same time, to be free of her.

Part of the Routledge Introductions to Contemporary Psychoanalysis series, this book is a must-read for psychoanalysts, students and scholars familiar with Lacan's ideas, as well as those approaching his theories for the first time. Lacan's unique and revolutionary understanding of human experience will benefit any scholar of human subjectivity, including art critics, cultural theorists, political commentators and academics in the humanities and social sciences.

Shlomit Yadlin-Gadot, PhD, is a psychoanalyst at the Tel Aviv Institute of Contemporary Psychoanalysis and Chair-Elect of the

Psychotherapy Program at Tel Aviv University. Her research focuses on Freud, Lacan and Truth, integrating perspectives of psychoanalysis, philosophy and cultural studies.

Uri Hadar is professor of psychology at Tel Aviv University and the Ruppin Academic Center. His fields of interest include psychoanalysis, nonverbal communication and the cerebral representation of natural language. His research and publications on psychoanalysis integrate Lacanian and Relational ideas.

Routledge Introductions to Contemporary Psychoanalysis

Aner Govrin, PhD, Series Editor
Yael Peri Herzovich, Executive Editor

"Routledge Introductions to Contemporary Psychoanalysis" is one of the prominent psychoanalytic publishing ventures of our day. It will comprise dozens of books that will serve as concise introductions dedicated to influential concepts, theories, leading figures, and techniques in psychoanalysis covering every important aspect of psychoanalysis.

The length of each book is fixed at 40,000 words.

The series' books are designed to be easily accessible to provide informative answers in various areas of psychoanalytic thought. Each book will provide updated ideas on topics relevant to contemporary psychoanalysis – from the unconscious and dreams, projective identification and eating disorders, through neuropsychoanalysis, colonialism, and spiritual-sensitive psychoanalysis. Books will also be dedicated to prominent figures in the field, such as Melanie Klein, Jaque Lacan, Sandor Ferenczi, Otto Kernberg, and Michael Eigen.

Not serving solely as an introduction for beginners, the purpose of the series is to offer compendiums of information on particular topics within different psychoanalytic schools. We ask authors to review a topic but also address the readers with their own personal views and contribution to the specific chosen field. Books will make intricate ideas comprehensible without compromising their complexity.

We aim to make contemporary psychoanalysis more accessible to both clinicians and the general educated public.

Aner Govrin, Editor

Donald Meltzer: A Contemporary Introduction
Meg Harris Williams

Projective Identification: A Contemporary Introduction
Robert Waska

For more information about this series, please visit: https://www.routledge.com/Routledge-Introductions-to-Contemporary-Psychoanalysis/book-series/ICP

Lacanian Psychoanalysis

A Contemporary Introduction

Shlomit Yadlin-Gadot and
Uri Hadar

Routledge
Taylor & Francis Group

LONDON AND NEW YORK

Designed cover image: © Michal Heiman, Asylum 1855–2020, The Sleeper
(video, psychoanalytic sofa and Plate 34), exhibition view, Herzliya Museum of
Contemporary Art, 2017.

First published 2023
by Routledge
4 Park Square, Milton Park, Abingdon, Oxon OX14 4RN

and by Routledge
605 Third Avenue, New York, NY 10158

Routledge is an imprint of the Taylor & Francis Group, an informa business

© 2023 Shlomit Yadlin-Gadot and Uri Hadar

British Library Cataloguing in Publication Data
A catalogue record for this book is available from the British Library

Library of Congress Cataloging-in-Publication Data
Names: Yadlin-Gadot, Shlomit, author. | Hadar, Uri, author.
Title: Lacanian psychoanalysis : a contemporary introduction / Shlomit Yadlin-
Gadot, Uri Hadar.
Description: New York, NY : Routledge, 2023. | Series: Routledge introductions
to contemporary psychoanalysis | Includes bibliographical references and index. |
Identifiers: LCCN 2022059110 (print) | LCCN 2022059111 (ebook) |
ISBN 9780367618704 (hardback) | ISBN 9780367618735 (paperback) |
ISBN 9781003106883 (ebook)
Subjects: LCSH: Psychoanalysis. | Lacan, Jacques, 1901-1981.
Classification: LCC BF173 .Y2393 2023 (print) | LCC BF173 (ebook) |
DDC 150.19/5--dc23/eng/20230415
LC record available at https://lccn.loc.gov/2022059110
LC ebook record available at https://lccn.loc.gov/2022059111

ISBN: 978-0-367-61870-4 (hbk)
ISBN: 978-0-367-61873-5 (pbk)
ISBN: 978-1-003-10688-3 (ebk)

DOI: 10.4324/9781003106883

Typeset in Times New Roman
by Taylor & Francis Books

To our patient and loved families

Contents

Figures

Acknowledgements

This book is a product of many years of friendship, of thinking, teaching and discussing Lacanian thought. We are grateful to the many friends, students and colleagues who had to bear with our delving into unfamiliar language, and that helped us lose and find ourselves in translation. To Aner Govrin for entrusting us with the task of writing this book and commenting on an earlier draft. And to Idan Oren for carefully reading and commenting on various parts of the book.

Preface

Why do we need another introductory text for the work of Lacan? Excellent books introduce and explain his ideas and legacy, for example Bowie (1991), Fink (1995), Dor (1998), Vanier (2000), Roudinesco (2014), Soler (2014), all of which have influenced our thinking. So why another one? The answer to this is twofold: Firstly, major thinkers are introduced differently as knowledge and perspectives keep changing. Secondly, any particular work must choose its singular emphases in theoretic fields that are of great breadth and complexity. On the whole, the present book takes the concepts and relation of subject-other to be the most fundamental determinants of Lacan's thought and our book reflects this in many ways.

Lacan is not the first psychoanalyst to create inextricable ties between subjectivity and otherness. Klein, Bion, Kohut and Winnicott had already deeply integrated contextuality into the subject's makeup. Yet, their thought is embedded in a realistic epistemological framework that distinguishes fantasy from reality. Lacan was a unique and innovative contributor to postmodernism and may be marked as the first to recast psychoanalysis in an intersubjective epistemology. Accordingly, he predicated the constitution of self[1] upon otherness in fateful ways that our book describes.

Three additional points comprise the singular nature of this introductory book. The *first* is our attempt to deliver Lacan's complex, abstract concepts in accessible language, illustrating them with contemporary, familiar examples. We do this alongside direct quotation from Lacanian texts, allowing readers to familiarize themselves with

Lacan's vernacular. The *second* is a certain freedom and novelty we allowed ourselves in our presentations. For example, Lacan presented several developmental ideas throughout his work, but was careful to avoid clear prescriptions of 'normal' development. Loyal to this commitment, we nevertheless systemized these ideas into an itinerary of child development, feeling that it may contribute immensely to the understanding of Lacanian thought. A *third* point concerns our belief that Lacanian ideas may enrich the thought and work of analysts from many schools, without demanding the adoption of Lacanian technique or methodology. We present the Lacanian subject, believing that it exists as a certain dimension in every contemporary subject, viewed from any theoretic perspective. His existential plight involves discovering both his subjugation to the other and the inherent liberating forces he may access. We remain close to psychoanalytic clinical journeys, but these ideas are presented also in their social expressions, which for Lacan are an inherent part of subjectivity. The same psychic forces that drive the subject's proclivity to addiction and painful relations with her[2] body also nurture such sub-cultures as Hollywood-inspired romance and Capitalist consumerism.

Lacan was a prolific and inventive writer. There are many words that he effectively invented and others which characterize his theory even though he did not invent them. It would be a feat to cover the entire Lacanian oeuvre of language and ideas, even in a frame much larger than the present one. We therefore had to make choices as to what terms and ideas we see as fundamental to Lacan's theory and heritage, but remain aware that others had made other choices. Of course, one cannot introduce Lacan without explaining such notions as the *signifier, the three orders, the centrality of language in shaping the unconscious*, etc. We discuss these in Chapters 1 and 2. In Chapter 3 we present aspects of subject development that shed light on the different orders in ways that semiotics does not. Chapter 4 elaborates on the *fundamental fantasy* and its relations with love, sexuality and consumerism. Chapter 5 describes Lacanian diagnostics that depart from definitions of pathology and health and focus on modes of desire and relations with others. Chapter 6, Sexuation, describes Lacan's startlingly contemporary definitions of gender, totally free from anatomy. Chapter 7 describes and explains Lacanian therapy in terms of objectives, techniques and ideas about individual involvement in shaping social reality. This last point leads to Chapter 8, where we discuss the manner in which Lacanian psychoanalysis can help understand the workings of politics and the ways individuals position themselves in it.

All-in-all the book gives a wide angle on Lacan and his work, offering ways in which the reader may be able to connect it to her or his personal reality. We hope this intention of ours materializes and that the informed reader will discover something new, while the uninformed reader will wish to know more.

Notes

1 Lacan did not use the term 'self'. We use it here as a reference to the concept of the first-person, as in colloquial speech.
2 Throughout the book, we shift between male and female gender of the un-marked person. Also, we shall capitalize words when used in their specific Lacanian manner.

Chapter 1

Background and Influences

To adequately appreciate and understand Lacan's contribution to psychoanalysis, one needs to know something about the context in which his thought developed and the prime thinkers who influenced him. We therefore set out by situating Lacan's writing in the turbulent passage from modern to postmodern thinking in post-WW2 Europe. In this context, Lacan tried to recast the Freudian subject – a relatively autonomous entity – with a subject who is always predicated upon an other. We describe Hegel's master-slave dialectic as Lacan's inspiration for this construal of the subject and outline the Sartrean touch that influenced his understanding of the relations between subject and other. We present Peirce's semiotics as the basis for Lacan's renowned 'orders': the Symbolic, Imaginary and the Real. We then briefly introduce Peirce's ideas of semiosis, the linguistic turn and Saussurian structuralism as background for Lacan's notion of the signifier and his transition from realistic epistemology to contextuality and language as determining factors of the subject. We end with Kojève's influence on Lacan's construal of desire, and begin, as any psychoanalytic thinking begins, with Freud.

1.1 The Freud connection

Lacan was a self-proclaimed Freudian. He made great efforts to retain the logic of the Freudian subject, yet he clearly departed Freud's commitment to two foundational anchoring points of modernity: The monadic Cartesian subject and the realistic

DOI: 10.4324/9781003106883-1

epistemology of science. The first envisions an isolated mind from which an external world arises, and the latter assumes an external environment that can be accurately perceived and differentiated from inner reality. This radical departure made Lacan's rereading of Freud into a unique school of thought, veiled by enigmatic, often obtuse, writing that subversively redefined basic Freudian concepts.

Freud remained loyal to the monadic aspect of the Cartesian subject yet overstepped the body-mind division when endowing him with an unconscious mind and a hysterical symptom. Roughly speaking, the Freudian unconscious – the **Id** – consists of innate and conflicting drives – the libido and the death drive. The drives are the infrastructure of mental life, characterized in terms of their bodily source, aim and object. The drive's *aim* is to achieve satisfaction through tension reduction and its *object* is that thing – body part, physical object or person – through which satisfaction is achieved under the guidance of the pleasure principle. The libido unfolds through the epigenetic, innate developmental sequence of oral, anal, phallic and Oedipal stages. Each stage manifests through bodily, erotogenic zones, through which satisfaction is created. Guided by the reality principle, the **Ego** develops from the Id, and is charged with reality-testing, balancing satisfaction with the safety of the organism. The maturation of the sexual drives involves a convergence of polymorphous partiality (connected with specific body parts) towards genital cohesion and a move from autoeroticism to object love. The resolution of the Oedipal complex and the creation of the **Super-ego** are conceptualized in terms of anatomy and family romance. This completes the Freudian tripartite *structural model* of the psyche in which the Ego negotiates instinctive, realistic and moral demands.

Lacan radically redefined the Freudian concepts he retained. When the Freudian ego becomes the Lacanian ego, it transforms from a trustworthy agency charged with self-preservation and reality-testing into a rigid, tricky symptom which distorts perception and creates narcissistic aggressivity, as we will later explain. In perpetual and heated debate with Ego-psychology and its emphasis on defense mechanisms and adaptation, Lacan remained adamantly loyal to the crucial positioning that Freud granted the unconscious in psychoanalytic theory. And yet, he thought of the unconscious as 'the discourse of the Other', giving it a linguistic character and thus markedly recasting the nature and dynamics of the drive. In Freud's view the origin of the unconscious and the entirety of the psyche is the **body** and the drive arises from it. In Lacan's view the origin of the unconscious is the **other** (we explain this in Chapter 3).

Freud challenged both the rationality of the Cartesian subject and the body-mind binary by introducing the drive, the unconscious and the hysterical symptom. And yet, in the Freudian scheme of things, the psyche must master its bodily progenitor. This reinstates *rationality* as a psychic ideal, grounded in the belief that *reality* may be known by the human mind. For Lacan, rationality is one sort of fiction and truth does not, indeed cannot, converge with knowledge.

1.2 The Continental connection and the linguistic turn

Lacan's major psychoanalytic contributions began in the wake of rationalism's catastrophic failure during WW2. Witnessing unimagined atrocities, philosophic thought determined that violence is inherent in Western metaphysics (Derrida 1974). This violence was grounded in an essentialist conception of a 'pure' subject and his logically predicated 'other'. The principles of *identity* and *totality* dangerously drew together the true and the ethical, informing rapacious violence towards otherness. From different directions, post-WW2 philosophies became heavily invested in re-thinking every aspect of the modern unified 'self' in its 'objective' reality, as both seemed hopelessly implicated in horrific violence and destruction. Existential thinkers like Heidegger (1962) and Sartre (1956), following Husserl's philosophic phenomenology, advocated a shift from essentialist categories (such as identity, binarism and objectivity) towards a subjective, existential basis for any possible knowledge. Foucault (1970), Derrida (1974) and Levinas (1990) continued this line of thinking, underlining its ethical derivatives. Born into a devout Christian family, Lacan began the life of a secular intellectual in a world bereft of divine goodness and truth.

He too needed to find a new ordering of subject and world, which amounted to a whole new tenet of living.

Lacan made language and speech the cornerstone of his approach to the psyche. The nodal positioning of language in Lacanian theory aligns with the 'linguistic turn', a kind of 'Other' – a theoretical environment – that Lacan was born into. The linguistic turn (Wittgenstein 1953, Heidegger 1962) conceived of language not as representing reality, but rather as constituting it. Reality is not only constructed through words and concepts, but also perceived through them. Words do not convey meanings external to them; they *form* meanings according to their own linguistic logic. Accordingly, all a person may know of himself and his world is mediated by and through language. The subject is born into a language that is always shared by a particular community. Consequently, she is always determined by the socio-linguistic context in which she lives. Her being is relative to the rules and norms of language, culture, society and community. Lacan's (1963–1964) definition of the subject as 'what one signifier represents for another signifier' fits snugly into the logic of the linguistic turn.

This logic amounts to a general and radical deconstruction of the subject, of truth, and binary notions of internal and external reality. Whereas the Freudian tripartite psyche was clearly differentiated from external reality, the Lacanian psyche is part of a larger field, formulated in terms of 'orders' or 'registers'. The fundamental structure in Lacanian psychoanalysis is the tripartite coexistence of three orders: The Real, the Imaginary and the Symbolic. These orders encompass inner and outer realities, undermining their mutual delineation. The interactions among the orders are dynamic and volatile throughout life and their conjoined effects constitute the subject and his reality. The knowledge of this very rough Lacanian scheme, even before explaining the related concepts in any detail, presents one of the main characteristics of the Lacanian subject: He himself is not a clearly delineated entity. He exists in and through a "force-field that traverses him" (Bowie 1991), where he is continuously formed and dissolved in relation with the other.

The *other*, as it unfolds across the three registers, precedes the subject and determines him. The subject is born into his parents' dreams and expectations, into social and linguistic conceptions and ideologies of subjecthood, which are well in place when he enters the scene. Their rules and specific modulating processes shape and forever remain part of the subject. For Lacan, *identity* can develop only by grappling with forms of otherness.

1.3 Dialectics and the other

Lacan drew on the Hegelian metaphor of master and slave as inspiration for the intertwining and irrevocable interdependence of self and other. In this well-known drama, Hegel (1807) described the process by which consciousness develops.[1] At first, self-consciousness is effectively a self-identity. In its desire for pure and complete existence, self-consciousness negates all otherness, consuming it within itself. This potentially endless process is checked when consciousness encounters another negating consciousness which *will not* be negated or consumed (Ibid, cl.175). Since self-conscious beings demand full and complete recognition, the ensuing dynamics is inevitably a life-and-death struggle. At its end, the two consciousnesses transform into two unequal beings: The master, who had been willing to risk his life, obtains recognition as an autonomous self-consciousness, while the slave, who surrendered in his desire to live, accepts his subservient status. *The master* now owns both the slave's consciousness and his own by virtue of the slave's recognition. He commits himself to pleasure, sending the slave to labor and provide his every desire. *The slave*, with his desires curbed and sublimated, works for his master. He develops through his interaction with the world, creating novel and complex modes of negation, but remains unrecognized. The master, progressively dissatisfied, becomes idle and captive of an inferior recognition. This dynamic, problematic for both master and slave, has only one resolution: Only mutual recognition may offer each consciousness true confirmation of being. Each mediates the other's existence, and it is possible for them to recognize themselves only as mutually recognizing entities (Ibid, cl.184).

While the other is necessarily tied up with the subject's constitution, their relations remain tense and volatile. Heidegger (1962) and Sartre (1956) gave existential, contemporary touches to this precarious interdependence. Heidegger's concept of Dasein as a 'being-in-the-world' was defined as a 'being-with-others' (Heidegger 1962, 112/119), a mode of living primordially entwined with care for others. But despite being primary in his world, others endanger Dasein's existence. Dasein is authentic only in the context of reflection, freedom and choice, but these may be compromised by 'falling prey to the world', i.e. adopting the common sense of 'Das Man' and a futile preoccupation with the world of others (Ibid, 164/ 176), which replaces the question of existence.

An additional version of these tense relations is given in Sartre's description of the objectifying effect of the other on the self. When one looks at an other, one sees his factual appearance, his existence as object. In the same manner, when an other gazes upon me, he relegates me to my being as an object, robbing me of my subjectivity. In Sartre's words: "... it is the recognition ... that I am indeed that object which the other is looking at ... I can be ashamed only as my freedom escapes me in order to become a given object" (Sartre 1956, p.261). Paradoxically, only when the subject is objectified and shamed does he perceive his freedom, and his being *beyond* an object. Only then " ... I see myself because somebody sees me ..." (Ibid, p.262). Optimistically, what ensues is the ability to realize that neither I nor the other are objects. These objectifying effects manifest strongly in Lacan's account of identity, whose first blueprint is given through the (m)other's alienating gaze (Chapter 3). Consequently, the subject's own desire objectifies others (Chapter 4). Becoming aware of these objectifying effects implies a profound responsibility for both subject and others.

1.4 Linguistic aspects: signs, semiosis and signifier

a. Charles Sanders Peirce

Peirce (1958) formulated an elaborate theory of signs and the manner in which they operate ('Semiotics'). He divided all signs into three categories: indexical, iconic and symbolic, differentiated by the degrees of freedom that exist between the sign and the idea it represents. *Indexical* signs have causal relations with their object and move along the single dimension of 'more' and 'less'. The thermometer, for example, indicates temperature through the expansion or contraction of liquid. *Iconic* signs have a figurative similarity to their object, as in a photograph. *Symbolic* signs are created purely by social convention, by agreement among people that, for example, the word 'bridge' signifies a solid passage over water. Lacan based his three orders on the semiotic works of Peirce (Muller 1996). The Peircian symbolic is almost identical to Lacan's, while his iconic resembles Lacan's Imaginary. The index-ical, however, is different from Lacan's Real. Peirce tried to create a representation that is closest to being simply an object, whereas Lacan's Real cannot be represented.

Peirce's theory of signification (Semiosis) seems also to have inspired Lacan's construal of relations among signifiers. Peirce's semiosis involves an additional triad: *Sign, object* and *interpretant.* In this triad, the *sign* represents its object (be it in indexical, iconic or symbolic mode). The *object* is the meaning of the sign. Here, Peirce differentiates the *Immediate object*, as represented in the sign, from the *Dynamic object*, the object's 'bedrock' existence (Peirce 1958). The *interpretant* is a development of the original sign through its understanding of the sign/object relation. Each interpretant allows an ever more complex understanding of the sign's object and drives the generation of additional inter-pretants. Any sign, by definition, must have the capacity to gen-erate an interpretant and any interpretant is a sign for the interpretant following it. This creates potentially infinite chains of signs, both proceeding and preceding from any given instance of signification. This, in turn, defines unique relations between the immediate and dynamic object. The immediate object is easily grasped as object represented in the sign, but the dynamic object, that is both its source and the eventual objective of semiosis, becomes a mythic, hypothetical entity, a Das Ding of sorts, never exhausted by the endless signifiers leading from and towards it (Yadlin-Gadot 2016).

This process of signification resonates Lacan's conception of the subject as a signifier gliding along endless chains of signifiers. Defining the subject as signifier does not entail reducing her materiality or raw reality. Rather, it places her as that dynamic object that can never be exhausted by signification and that is forever in the process of becoming in the many modes of the Symbolic. In general, the Lacanian signifier is always rooted in a Thing, but it also makes that Thing irretrievably lost, once processes of representation and signification begin. Signification will always lead away from the Thing while, at the same time, trying to reach it. In the process of this tragic and Sisyphean quest, the subject discovers a world of meanings that she created and for which she bears responsibility.

b. Ferdinand de Saussure

Lacan's ideas drew from the work of Ferdinand de Saussure (Saussure 1915), the revolutionary founder of modern linguistics. Saussure defined language as an essentially social phenomenon, an arbitrarily structured system of agreed-upon signs. Each sign consists of an arbitrary, inseparable conjoining of signifier (sound, shape or pattern) and signified (concept). Roughly, the sign's value is created by its difference from other signs along two basic axes: A paradigmatic (metaphorical) axis, and a syntagmatic (metonymic) axis. The former refers to the manner in which signs can replace each other, while the latter refers to the manner in which they join together, side-by-side. These definitions give rise to language's most basic characteristic: Meaning is created merely by virtue of difference. As such, it is *inherent* to language, without needing an external world to which meanings correspond. Saussure differentiated *langue* or 'language' – the linguistic system – from *parole*, 'speech', which consists of individual speakers and hearers delivering communicative messages between them. Langue is strictly rule-governed, while parole allows deviations that may gradually alter the rules.

Lacan drew from Saussure the idea that man is born into langue in ways that confine possibilities of parole, of expression. Language creates the possibility for thought and expression, but it also creates the contingencies that restrict it. The Saussurean system is arbitrary in the sense that the rules could be different. For example, the letter 'peh' in Hebrew acts sometimes as 'f' and sometimes as 'p', but when it appears as the first letter in a word it is *always* a 'p'. This rule is arbitrary: It did not have to be so. This idea was crucial for Lacan: Language has no natural or godly source. (Wo)man is its origin, but she is also its product, its sole creator and slave. In order to live in her own mind and social settings, (wo)man must recognize their law which, in turn, is given to change. Law is a form of 'Das Man' from which an 'I' may evolve. In addition, as with Saussure, meanings develop through the creation of endless complex chains of signifiers, glued together by the operations of metonymy and metaphor. However, Lacan's revolutionary move in relation to Saussure was loosening the bonds between signifier and signified and granting precedence to the signifier. The Lacanian signifier always marks both presence and absence.

All–in–all, for Lacan man lives in the realm of arbitrary hierarchies of law and language, called 'the Other' (or 'the big Other'). The social forces and structures that shape man reflect the Other's demands. Man also lives among (uncapitalized, specular) others as peers: Rivals and reflections, enemies and lovers (like the Hegelian entities that mutually recognize each other). Is there anything *of the subject* that precedes or exceeds o/Otherness? The Lacanian answer is given in the nature of a search.

1.5 Connecting desire, the other and language

Lacanian being is constructed through, and by means of, *desire*, *otherness* and *language*. This is concisely formulated by Lacan's contemporary, Kojève:

> Man becomes conscious of himself at the moment ... he says 'I'. To understand man by understanding his 'origin' is, therefore, to understand the origin of the 'I' revealed by speech ... The Desire of a being is what constitutes that being as I and reveals it as such by moving it to say I.
>
> (Kojève 1969, p.3)

Moreover, "Human desire must be directed toward another desire ... That is why human reality can only be social ... society is human only as a set of desires mutually desiring one another as desire" (Kojève 1969, p.6). On a more personal note, Kojève states that "to desire the desire of another is, in the final analysis, to desire that the value that I am or that I 'represent' be the value desired by the other" (Ibid).

For Kojève, the master-slave struggle centers upon the government of desire. The master becomes totally dependent on his slave to supply his desired objects. Yet, and more importantly, the objects also create and maintain the desire of the slave by *perpetuating his frustration*. The slave gradually comes to govern the satisfaction or suspension of the master's desire, and thus controls both the world in which he labors *and* the master's desire. Since the value of desire increases by being repeatedly deferred and displaced, *the question of ownership of objects becomes secondary to the question of owning the other's desire*. One may want to completely absorb the other's desire, be its ultimate object and thereby own it, but since that is impossible, desire is endless and has no true object that may ever satiate it. This is what keeps subjectivity moving from object to object in its quest to arouse the other's desire. The subject endlessly tries to ensure the possession of an object that will promise him the other's desire. Inevitably he fails. The Lacanian subject, like the Kojèvian one, is subjugated to the beauty and tragedy of being forever bound to the desire of the other.

Defining desire for the other's desire as constitutional of subjectivity effectively draws the infrastructure of the non-essential subject. The positivity of the Freudian drive is replaced by the negativity of Lacanian desire. The bedrock of biological elements is displaced by otherness, while sexuality as anatomy or destiny is displaced by Symbolic *sexuation* (see Chapter 6). Forms of development – seemingly epigenetic and predetermined – are in actuality governed by social rules, recognized as arbitrary. Identity becomes an Imaginary construct, divorced of any primordial, extra-linguistic or extra-social element. The core of the subject is a *lack*.

The above construal emphasizes the existential dilemmas that occupy the Lacanian subject and are set as challenges for Lacanian psychoanalysis: Can the subject admit the lack that constitutes her core and accept it? Can she give up the task of making herself whole, a task doomed for frustration? Can she extricate herself from the position of being (or wanting to be) the exclusive object of the other's desire? Can she face the terror of acknowledging that the ordered system that formed her is arbitrary? Having gone that far, does she dare to transgress the law of this order? In the end, the prime question of the Lacanian subject is a question of being, of subjectification, of testing the limits of representation in order to find an anchorage in the particularity of the Real.

Note

1 There are two accepted interpretations of the master-slave allegory. The first sees it as depicting a drama enacted within one consciousness. The second, which we take up, depicts a drama enacted between two distinct agencies.

Chapter 2

The Lacanian Orders

Lacan defines three orders, or registers, through which the subject and his world are given and organized: The Symbolic, the Imaginary and the Real. The Symbolic and the Imaginary are orders of representation, whereas the Real is an order of everything that evades representation and meaning. This gap is fundamental to the general predicament of mental life, as some of its most powerful phenomena cannot be described. For purposes of clarity we present each order separately, though they are forever inextricably knotted.

2.1 The Symbolic order

The Symbolic is first and foremost a representational order, structured by an arbitrary *law*. Language best incarnates the Symbolic order's essence, but it encompasses many inter-related subsystems that form organized society, such as norms, morality, institutions, and culture.[1] For example, the social family structure is governed by rules of hierarchy that differentiate parents and children. Parents represent authority and children have to listen to them. Yet, parents can't demand that children harm themselves, because another family rule defines family members as responsible for each other's well-being. They cannot demand it also because the family is embedded in a larger social organization, such as the state, that also formulates laws, such as the law protecting children from parental abuse. It is a major tenet of Lacan's work that the Symbolic in its entirety, as a complex network of rule-governed

DOI: 10.4324/9781003106883-2

interconnected sub-systems, is as pertinent to the child as her family.

Each system, linguistic or social, is constituted by certain basic elements. For example, *words* and phonemes are elementary units of language, while *individuals* are elementary units of the family. The Symbolic's basic elements are **signifiers**. Lacan, in a dramatic move, put words and individuals on par as signifiers, thus strongly illustrating the logic of the Symbolic. Whilst Saussure's signifier is tied up with a fairly fixed meaning ('the signified'), Lacan's signifier is constrained, yet shifts along high degrees of freedom and changes dramatically across contexts. Consider Lacan's fine example concerning the words 'ladies' and 'gentlemen' that seem to have fairly fixed and simple meanings. But written on a rectangular sign in a train station alongside an arrow, they most probably mean 'toilets'. When meaning is asserted in a particular context, other meanings remain occluded unless a shift of perspective is produced. In analytic psychotherapy we induce such shifts, enabling other meanings to emerge.

The individual is a signifier in terms of his place in the social structure. A group of individuals create a family, if recognized as parents and children. For Lacan, family is not a matter of blood relations. The necessary and sufficient condition for being a family member is registration in the relevant census. Thus, registered, adopted children are on par with biological children as 'siblings'. The 'firstborn child' is a signifier that defines a place in the family: Son to his parents and elder to his siblings and, in some societies, bearer of inheritance rights. These properties cannot be observed. They represent the fact that the individual belongs to a particular social structure – his nuclear family – which is embedded in a larger social structure ruled by certain laws of property and ownership.

The Old Testament represents this neatly. Esav and Jacob were the sons of Itzhak and Rivka. Rivka, favoring her second son Yaacov, instructed him to impersonate Esav and to deceive his father in order to receive the blessing given to the first-born. The ruse irrevocably granted Jacob the status and privileges of first-born. This biblical story resonates an earlier one in which Abel 'purchased' the status of first-born by deviously taking advantage of his elder brother's hunger when returning from work in the fields. The Bible illustrates that being 'first-born' is not a fact of 'reality'. It is a signifier that can shift by *contract*. This renders Lacan's enigmatic sentence comprehensible: "*The signifier ... represents a subject to another signifier*" (Lacan 1972–1973, p.49). When we look to each other we see 'students', 'teachers', 'Brahmins', 'Jews'. We attach worlds of meaning to these signifiers, telling us who these individuals are, what they are allowed to do, think or say. We may derive our relations with other members of society long before meeting them.

The signifier never exhausts or completely defines the subject. The individual is forever unique and elusive, sliding along the signifiers that define her: Female, child, dancer, boss. Lacan emphasizes this elusiveness *alongside* the fact that, more than we realize, we are determined and governed by the signifiers that mark our place in the social world. We *are* to a large extent what society makes us out to be. My life is strongly influenced by the meaning society attaches to the signifier 'woman' or 'Jew'. I may be, for example, a recognized subject or my husband's property.

Meaning is created and transformed by combining signifiers into chains, following conventional rules of different kinds (linguistic, ethical, etc.). Syntactic rules determine combinations admissible in language. 'John wanted to go home' is an admissible sentence, while 'home John to wanted go' is not. Still, sentences containing violations could be meaningfully incorporated into poetic structures. Now, take the sentence 'shoot that prisoner'. It is syntactically admissible, but ethic rules (hopefully) make it inadmissible. Foucault calls this complex interaction among rules an *épistémè*: "In any given culture ... one *épistémè* ... defines the conditions of possibility of all knowledge, whether expressed in a theory or ... practice" (Foucault 1970, p.183). Everything we know, indeed *may* know, of ourselves and the world is shaped by society's explicit and implicit rules. Lacan calls them 'the law'. Since rules have an arbitrary dimension, they may be violated or changed.

Symbolic signifiers, as shown above, are 'empty' in that they carry no inherent meaning, but rather create meaning through joining into *chains*. Chains of signifiers are meaningful when joined according to rules of combination and hierarchy, which Lacan calls, respectively, 'metonymy' and 'metaphor'.[2] And yet, through practice or experience, signifiers often become strongly attached to particular meanings that Lacan calls 'quilting points' (*point de capiton*). Some quilting points are socially-determined (dictionaries permanently attach signified and signifier), while others vary among people. Thus, for one person 'dog' may signify 'man's best friend', while for another it signifies 'dangerous beast'. 'Home' may be the safest or, alternatively, the most dangerous place on earth. In a world of empty signifiers ordered by arbitrary rules, quilting points serve the crucial function of anchoring meaning. Lacan, with his proclivity to equations and abstractions, believed he could figure the minimum number of quilting points needed to provide an individual with a sense of sanity and stability. For all subjects, as we will explain shortly, the 'name-of-the-father' (*nom du père*) functions as a quilting point that irrevocably weds desires with words. This situates the basic principles of Oedipal law – prohibiting murder and incest – as cornerstones of society's structure.

The object of the Symbolic order is the big Other (identified by a capital 'O' ('A' in French, for 'Autre')), consisting of language, law and social structure. For Lacan, the Other is also the *unconscious*, defined as 'the discourse of the Other'. This may seem a paradox, with 'Other' referring to both external social structure *and* the innermost unconscious. However, for Lacan this is a nodal point, because external and internal are not fixed locations. They are dynamic moments that can shift in accordance with mental states. Thus, on the syntactic level, the Other as unconscious is also subject to rules of metaphor and metonymy (condensation and displacement). On the semantic level, it defines our unconscious as seething with our parents' discourse and desire. Long before we appear on the scene, our parents imagined and dreamt our existence. The name they chose for us (e.g., after a deceased brother or parent) holds their hopes and anxieties. Their childhood imagination of themselves as parents is ingrained in our flesh. This ongoing discourse of our parents with themselves, with each other, with their own parents and significant others is the stuff of which our unconscious is made. We are unaware of this. It is a knowledge without a subject, which operates on us and determines us as subjects. Included here are also the endless explicit and implicit social restrictions that we have incorporated, much like the mostly unconscious Freudian superego.

This for Lacan is the Symbolic part of the unconscious, coded in signifiers that both convey and conceal meaning. The subject has blind areas created by his semiotic habits, which may have been formed by trauma or by social conventions. These determine not only unconscious life, but also our ways of construing reality. For Lacan, the unconscious lends itself to interpretation but, more importantly, *the unconscious interprets*. The world lacks metaphysical underpinnings – realistic or divine – so reality can only be unconsciously understood. Reality is constructed by encoded desires and fears, both our own and of others.

2.2 The Imaginary order

The Imaginary is an order of representation that relies on sense information, mostly visual. The object determines its representation in ways that cohere with its physicality, in contradistinction to Symbolic representation, where an **arbitrary** element always exists. The word 'ball', for example, is purely Symbolic inasmuch as there is no similarity or organic connection between the word and the object. By distinction, the drawing of a ball, however schematic, always bears a similarity to its object, as in the following picture: ☉

This is, then, an Imaginary representation of a ball.

Being faithful to the object's physicality restricts the Imaginary representation in the degrees of freedom along which it can change. The drawing may be larger or smaller, colorful or given against different backgrounds, etc., but it must retain its main defining features. The Imaginary may include auditory/olfactory representations, like waves in the sea, but visual forms dominate Imaginary representation due to their relative wealth.

The mirror stage, described in the next chapter, is the point of entry into the Imaginary. It describes the moment that the child encounters his reflection in the mirror and jubilantly identifies with it. A huge gulf lies between the mirror image and the child's fluid, disjoint self-experiencing at the time of this first encounter. Yet, the coherence and illusion of control given in the image's gestalt, alongside the exuberant directive of a validating Other ('look at my beautiful baby in that mirror!'), lure the child into identifying with it. This divorces (and frees) him from fragmented bodily experience and provides him with the first blueprint of identity, the core of his Imaginary, *conscious ego*. The ego holds for the subject a relatively stable and coherent image of himself, which allows him to orient in the world. But Lacan marks its inherently *invalid and alienated* character as paradigmatic of the Imaginary order. Our senses lead us into illusions.

The dynamic involved in identity's initial constitution is so fundamental to the child's sense of self that it gets generalized. It becomes an overarching ability to create images, remember and use them in negotiating the demands of life. Imaginary representations, like Symbolic ones, can create chains of signifiers. Some images become trapped in the unconscious and surface, for example, in dreams. Further generalizing from his mirror image, the child identifies also with those who are close and similar to him, especially other children. This may serve as the primitive base of empathy, but it carries a dangerous counterpart – collapsing the essential differentiation between self and another. In this sense, for Lacan, the ego's knowledge always carries a paranoid edge – I am never quite myself and the other is never quite herself.

The identification with the mirror image and the impact of the Imaginary is not a one-time infantile folly. As we experience deep into adulthood, self-experiencing is often determined by our mirror reflection. We awake every morning disgruntled, hazy and un-oriented. We stare blankly at the blurry off-putting person reflected in the mirror. As we shower, dress, fix our hair and adjust our makeup, we gradually reposition and re-insert ourselves in our body. We gradually find in the mirror the familiar self we recognize. The recognized self is not the one who startled us when we first woke up. It is the groomed, held-together self that we trust to go out in the world and represent us. It assures us that our anxieties are not manifest on our face, that our various dream selves, still on the edge of consciousness, do not give themselves away. Oftentimes in the morning, and by no means by chance, the moment we adjust our mirror image is also the moment we forget our dreams. In this sense, every morning we re-enact the mirror stage, bidding our authentic, fragmented body-self goodbye and transforming ourselves into a mastered gestalt.

Imaginary claims on ourselves have gone a step further in our era. The culture of selfies, Instagram and story apps keeps us in a perpetual state of visual reflection. Taking a picture of ourselves abroad, we see *inside the photo* how beautiful the view is. We don photogenic smiles to create the enthused traveler we would like to be in the eyes of imagined others viewing the pictures. WhatsApp 'filters' alter and better appearance. A young woman may take the processed WhatsApp image to her plastic surgeon and instruct him to adjust her face accordingly. Giving way to the lure of the Imaginary, she might sacrifice her face's expression and unique curiosities. While reality is forever heterogeneous and fluid, Imaginary representation accords with apperception, rendering objects distinct and complete. In this way, it freezes and simplifies the complex, dynamic nature of both self and reality, trading them in for an Imaginary, false sense of security in the form of permanence and stability.

In striving for similarity and completeness, the Imaginary always reduces the object. The simplest reduction results from the gap between the three-dimensionality of physical objects and the two-dimensionality of iconic representation. We also create Imaginary representations of people, necessarily reducing their complexity, often collapsing difference and hurriedly assuming common, shared features with ourselves. Saying 'I know exactly how you feel', we are unaware of claiming a knowledge that necessarily negates that which defines the other as 'other'. We pair with others we deem similar and experience betrayal when the other's difference surfaces.

The logic of the Imaginary is dyadic. The object is always, primarily, an object of identification, given in the measure of the subject. The Imaginary 'me' always involves comparison to others and, with it, rivalry. Jointly with the ego's low tolerance to difference, otherness in itself becomes experienced as threatening. The other, when *not* serving as my image, endangers me and destabilizes my ability to know and recognize myself. This dynamic creates hostility of the kind that Klein's (1946) 'paranoid schizoid' position describes. It is portrayed in numerous fictional 'doubles', trapped in dynamics of 'either me or you'. From Abel and Cain to Batman and The Joker, these relations of doubles always hold parameters of identification and negation, a rivalry that may be resolved only by obliterating the other, yet never quite gets there because annihilating the other results in the annihilation of the undifferentiated self. For Lacan, this is more than an intersubjective dynamic. It is the general logic of madness in its demand for total presence (reminiscent of Hegel's negating self-consciousness). "Not only the madness that lies behind the walls of asylums, but also the madness that deafens the world with its sound and fury" (Lacan 1949, p.7). For Lacan the characteristics of the Imaginary – the striving for certainty, totality and unity – fuel the constitution of totalitarian regimes and their crimes of purification.

In his analysis of the Imaginary, Lacan simultaneously denies the possibility of total presence and recognizes the human need for it. Only a different form of logic can redeem this volatile dynamic from its inherent instability. This other logic is provided by the Symbolic order. Symbolic representation is triadic and based on difference. It may avoid being oppressive by recognizing both difference and the Imaginary tendency to obliterate the gap between self and other.

2.3 The order of the Real

While the Symbolic and the Imaginary are orders of representation whose nature is fairly well-known to us, the Real is by definition *unknowable*. It includes the subject's most basic and immediate bodily experience. Lacan defines the Real as the cause (*tuche*) that drives the forces of inexhaustible representation. On the other hand, we never know what it *is*. In that sense, it is quite similar to Kant's (1781) 'das ding an sich': the thing in itself. And indeed, in referring to the 'Thing', or 'Das Ding', Lacan is always referring to the Real.

The 'Thing' in Lacan's terminology is the primal, prehistoric, unforgettable Other, which the subject imagines as a supreme, albeit unnamable, good. This primal object is associated with the pre-Oedipal Mother or, more precisely, with the 'dark continent' of the maternal body: "The whole development of psycho-analysis ... at the level of mother/child inter-psychology ... is nothing more than an immense development of the essential character of the maternal thing, of the mother, insofar as she occupies the place of that thing, of das Ding" (Lacan 1959–1960, p.67). The Thing, the maternal body, is at first neither Imaginary nor Symbolic. It exists as a Real fullness of *jouissance*, which is an extreme bodily pleasure, bordering on pain. This is the experience of ultimate and ecstatic fullness that cannot be symbolized and that we may get a taste of in such liminal experiences as orgasm, religious exaltation, psychotropic 'trips', etc.

As an experience, the Real is uncanny, traumatic, ineffable and uncontrollable, but it can also be experienced as extreme physical sensations of pleasure and pain (*jouissance*). It usually involves a primordial stratum of mental life, eruptions of turbulent impulses (resonant of Freud's partial, polymorphic drives) that may appear as markings on the body (e.g., stigmata). The Real is the touché, the cause and driving force of signification, the Thing that gives rise to the lived-in world of phenomena.

In the spirit of Freud's negation, Lacan defined the Real as everything in mental life that does *not* fall in the realm of the Symbolic and the Imaginary. The Real evades representation, but its *influence* can be represented in various ways, just as the Freudian drive may never be directly observed except through its derivatives. We cannot represent the Real, but its workings leave traces, indications and effects, manifest in symptoms, trauma and *jouissance*, and in the experience of absences or gaps in Imaginary or Symbolic representation. For an attentive person, experience is saturated with these kinds of gaps. In the face of the Real "... all words cease and all categories fail" (Lacan 1962–1963, p.164).

Freud differentiated fear and *anxiety*, claiming that anxiety has no object. In fear we know what we are afraid of. It may be pain or injury, some threatening object or person, or an aversive event. But our anxiety seems to lack a definite reason. Lacan (Ibid) deems this distinction imprecise: Anxiety has an object, but it resides unknowable in the Real. In this way, the un-representable Real functions as the 'object of anxiety par excellence'. This explains the intractability of anxiety, as the subject can do very little with it.

In Lacan's analysis of Freud's 'Irma' dream, he describes the encounter with the Real as embodied in the visual image of Irma's infected throat. Freud describes the infection in great detail and the reader can almost perceive (or *sense*) Irma's throat. Lacan describes it as:

> ... a horrendous discovery ..., the flesh one never sees, the foundation of things, the other side of the head, of the face, the secretory glands par excellence, the flesh from which everything exudes, at the very heart of mystery, the flesh inasmuch as it is suffering, is formless ... [This is a] specter of anxiety ... the final revelation of you are this – You are this which is so far from you, this which is the ultimate formlessness.
> (Lacan 1954–1955, p.145)

In the dream, Freud encounters the exposure of material being that no symbol can ameliorate. We may encounter this when injured, or when the unknown insides of our body are revealed.

The persistence of symptoms is explained by Lacan by reference to the symptom's Real 'core'. Analysis alleviates symptoms by interpreting their symbolic significance. Yet often, the symptom (and the dream, as described above) contain an uninterpretable element that is not meaning-dependent and is therefore resistant to therapeutic intervention. Consider, for example, the case of Anna O (Breuer & Freud 1895). Her bodily symptoms alleviated considerably when she recalled related episodes from her father's illness. But they never quite vanished. They kept shifting from one bodily site to another, embodying this un-symbolized 'remainder', a core of the Real that persisted in her, in her body, her way of life.

Generally speaking, traces of the Real may often be tied up with the body or bodily experience: "... once something of the Real comes to be known, there is something lost; and the surest way to approach this something lost is to conceive of it as a fragment of the body" (Lacan 1962–1963, p.3). This does not mean that the body as such is just Real. Not at all. It is as Symbolic and Imaginary as it is Real. Indeed, the mirror stage is all about the body as Imaginary and we can all name body parts, so it is Symbolic just as well. But the way that the Real presents itself tends to involve the body. Consider, for example, panic attacks that occur after recognizable triggers and vanish in a similarly mysterious way. They include accelerated heartbeat, shortness of breath and the blurring of vision, despite the fact that the related systems may be fully functional.

Art often, in various ways, tries to evoke the Real. Consider, for example, a well-known scene from Joseph Conrad's book, *Heart of Darkness* (Conrad 1902). The protagonist, Marlow, joins an expedition through the Congo's unexplored jungles. Well into the trip, the expedition encounters a small colony ruled with immense violence by a European called Kurtz. Marlow describes how he experienced Kurtz when the latter conveyed his African experience: "Anything approaching the change that came over his features I have never seen before and hope never to see again. He cried in a whisper at some image, at some vision – he cried out twice, a cry that was no more than a breath: 'The horror! The horror!'" (Note the equation between the phrase and the bodily act of breathing.) The phrase is often interpreted as expressing the sense of evil that had seeped into Kurtz's African endeavor. In our reading, it also indicates the reason for Kurtz's venture into the Congo: the pursuit of the Real; the urgent need to master forces that are essentially beyond control.

Saul Bellow's *Henderson the Rain King* (Bellow 1959) describes more explicitly the protagonist's need to contact this unmediated dimension of existence. Henderson, utterly disgusted with a life dedicated to pursuit of meaning, travels to Africa. In Africa, he contacts bodily experience in intimate and invigorating ways. This extends beyond Henderson's body to Willatale's body, a tribal queen holding him prisoner. Henderson describes his sensations when made to touch her belly with his face:

> I was aware of the old lady's navel and her internal organs as they made sounds of submergence. I felt as though I was riding in a balloon above the Spice Islands, soaring in hot clouds while exotic odors arose from below. My own whiskers pierced me inward, in the lip.

> (Bellow 1959, p.74)

There is a clear movement to-and-fro between the body of other and subject, primordially undifferentiated, both experienced in the Real.

2.4 The relationships between the orders

Despite the ability to characterize separately the differential logic of the three orders and their mental, emotional and experiential corollaries, they are inextricably connected in the Lacanian universe. Lacan used mathematical theories of knots to represent this, one of which is the 'Borromean knot' (Lacan 1972–1973). A simple representation of this appears in Figure 2.1.

The knot presents how the disappearance of one order (ring in the diagram) causes the whole structure – representing the entirety of world and experience – to crumble. In mental life the experiential counterpart of the structure's dissolution is catastrophic, psychotic disorientation, a chaotic dissociation of words and images from meanings.

The knotting illustrates that any element of mental life exists across all three registers and expresses itself in modes particular to each. The first and most immediate illustration of this is the subject. Each person is Symbolic in the places she holds in social structures and their derivative meanings. In her Symbolic identity, she may be an American, Muslim, a sister and spouse, a teacher, etc., all at the same time. These Symbolic elements reflect categories relevant to our day and age: gender and familiar roles, nationality

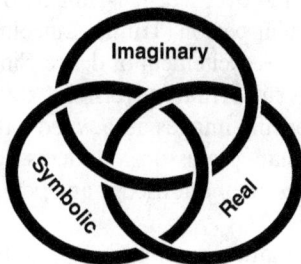

Figure 2.1 The Borromean Knot of Orders

and religion, formal positions authorized by different sets of rules. Most aspects of Symbolic identity are recorded in various rosters that can be traced and witnessed from a third-person perspective.

In the Symbolic I am also a subject of my unconscious, meaning that I am determined by certain signifiers and discourses of which I am unaware that structure my unconscious ways of construing reality. One is Symbolic also as a desiring being – a nodal point developed in the next chapter. Imaginary identity involves one's familiar self and body-image, her conscious stream of thought and feeling. It also includes Imaginary-based, narcissistic hostilities, rivalries and ways of falling in love. The Real dimension of self tends to involve uncanny bodily experience, including skin abnormalities, intense pleasure bordering on pain, squeamish or nauseous responses to images of the inside of the body or its injuries. It might appear as a tingling down one's back, a sense of being watched or followed, states of depersonalization or de-realization.

One's 'self' is a combined totality of these dimensions, differentially experienced at different moments or contexts, when a particular dimension becomes more dominant than others. Awaiting one's turn in passport control, one becomes 'a citizen of the state'. During orgasm, one's Real exalted experiences may overshadow other dimensions. A fight with one's teenage daughter may tax one's ability to contain aggression or accommodate interpersonal differences in the Imaginary. In principle, it is not only persons that have order-specific dimensions, but every social entity. For example, 'The US presidency' has a Symbolic, constitutional dimension that is rule-governed; it is Imaginary inasmuch as it is inhabited by a particular person (Trump, Lincoln, etc.); and it is Real inasmuch as it generates excitement or desire. Similarly, 'a university' is Symbolic in the rules that govern its status and operation, Imaginary in the specific images associated with it (its geographic location, its particular professors, students, etc.), and Real in embodying the *jouissance* of knowledge and being embodied in flesh, concrete or steel.

Even the paradigmatic Symbolic entity – the 'signifier' – has Imaginary and Real dimensions. It is Symbolic in its semantic 'emptiness' and syntactic ability to connect with other signifiers,

Imaginary in being associated with a paradigmatic image, or in being wedded to a fixed signified, and Real in its physical properties such as sound (if spoken) or shape (if written or drawn).

Notes

1 Language is any system of signs that follows arbitrary rules that may be rendered explicit, even when not consciously known by the linguistic group's members.

2 Lacan saw these two axes as equivalent to Freud's 'primary processes' of displacement and condensation. Formulating them in linguistic terms was more than a point of semantics. It was part of his project of de-essentializing psychoanalytic thought and elaborating on his conception of the (de-anatomized) unconscious as 'Discourse of the Other'.

Chapter 3

The Logic of Development, Desire and Jouissance

Lacan never presented his ideas in the form of a developmental theory given in traditional timeframes.[1] He avoided this so as not to prescribe a fixed, 'normative' course of development that would suggest that there are 'proper' ways to think, feel or develop. Nevertheless, Lacan did formulate 'logical moments' in the subject's constitution. This means that we cannot account for the subject unless we assume that he had gone through certain moments and incorporated their effects in his person. We take the liberty of ordering these 'logical moments', believing that this sort of presentation helps clarify aspects of Lacan's theorizing in ways that other perspectives do not (Yadlin-Gadot 2021). Especially, we aim to explain a number of developmental issues: a) That all crucial moments in the subject's constitution are critically influenced by an other; b) How the logic of the representational orders derives from the logical developmental moments; c) How desire and jouissance are understood by reference to these moments; d) The way in which Lacan's therapeutic technique is construed in relation to developmental logic.

3.1 The mirror stage

Our developmental account begins with Lacan's thought experiment, motivated by actual observation of the infant's encounter with her mirror image. Lacan, like Freud, emphasized the radical prematurity of the newborn human infant as a formative dimension of human ontogenesis. More than any other mammal, the

DOI: 10.4324/9781003106883-3

human infant is born uncoordinated, vulnerable and insufficient, unable to perform behaviors that ensure her survival. That makes her totally reliant on others for feeding, keeping warm, avoiding dangers, etc. The newborn experiences herself as torn and exiled from the mother's body, a perforated bundle of fluid, chaotic and disjoint sensations. In this terrifying realm of disintegration, the infant is offered her mirror image and encouraged to identify with it. Magically, instantly, validated by the Other's reflecting activity, she recognizes herself in the mirror as a whole, *identified* unit that may encompass and contain her in an upright gestalt.

Of course, Lacan says, the infant's recognition of herself in this imago involves an absurd 'misrecognition' and entails a deep alienation. The infant's brand-new sense of coherence and identity conceals the fact that it is derived from something external to herself and that a huge gulf lies between the imago and her own authentic disintegrated bodily experiencing. Furthermore, the imago is suffused with the discourse and desire of the Other ('Look at you! You are as pretty as mamma, strong as papa!'). The signifiers of this other's discourse carry Symbolic meanings, Imaginary descriptions and emotional effects in the Real, all of which are branded in the infant's psyche and flesh, forming the contingent basis of his being. As Lacan sees it, the need to answer the question 'Who am I?' is a pressing one, indicating a subversive human striving towards identity. The mirror-image identity feels by far superior to authentic, fragmented body experiencing, also accounting for the infant's jubilant response.

Note that the first marking of Lacanian identity does not rely on the experience of the actual *body*, but rather on an *externally-derived body image*. Indeed, in order to identify with the upright coherent image, a clear break from authentic bodily experience must occur. Nothing here can be made better by adequate parental mirroring or holding. Identity is predicated on a fundamental alienation that splits the child's organic experience from his initial representation. Instead of an essential core, a bodily or 'true' self, Lacan presents the body *image*, alias Imaginary 'ego', as the primary form of identity. The ego is a hoax, a fraud. It constructs unity, coherence and illusion of boundaries for the sake of self and Other's recognition. Thus, the ego – created in the visual modality and based on misrecognition – is the paradigmatic form of Lacan's Imaginary order.

And yet, the ego's importance must not be understated. It provides an experience of envelope and container (akin to Anzieu's 'skin-ego' (Anzieu 2016)). It separates 'inside' from 'outside' and forecloses experiences of fragmentation and open-endedness. With time, this perfect, coherent image (which Lacan (1949) called 'Ideal ego') begins to arouse envy in the child and he seeks to own it and put himself in its place. Moreover, the child feels that the image is there to usurp him, as he himself had assumed the imago as his own. In cycles of introjection and projection, a basic paranoid positioning is created, boiling down to the binary choice and logic of the Imaginary: 'It's me or you'. These intense relations of love, hate and narcissistic rivalry, in which self and other are never quite differentiated, remain a paradigmatic dimension of future relationships that Lacan calls 'narcissistic aggressivity'. These relations are tempered by the entrance into the triadic space of the Symbolic, with the resolution of the Oedipal complex.

3.2 Oedipal development

The Lacanian Oedipal complex consists of three successive moments. At first, mother and child are given in a state of pure presence, timelessness and formlessness. The infant is immersed in a maternal sensuous matrix – unable to distinguish self and (m)other. In this situation, mother and infant only exist in unity and are neither dead nor alive when apart.[2] The experience here is boundless, an 'oceanic feeling' (Freud 1930), an intermixture of pleasure and pain, life and death (Parsons 1999). To maintain it and its accompanying jouissance – the child seeks to ensure that he is mother's exclusive object of desire, that nothing will lure her away from him. With the desire of both mother and infant seemingly satisfied, an imaginary wholeness is created and no lack exists. This is a curious position, as we shall soon see, for the Lacanian subject is defined by his desire. Desire, in turn, is by definition, a form of lack. When one lacks nothing, one desires nothing. So where is the subject at this moment? He is in the positive Real(m) of jouissance, 'not on the side of the subject', not yet on the side of the negativity of desire.

This first moment delivers us (as readers) to a classic Freudian formulation, which serves as a starting point for diverging ideas. Freud (1933) described the development of femininity in the conventional heterosexual scheme as entailing a displacement of the little girl's early attachment from mother to father. What drives the girl's disengagement from her mother is her terrible disappointment with her. She recognizes that mother is damaged (with no penis) and, even worse, has transferred this damage to her. The resentful, angry little girl turns to her better-equipped father, hoping that someday he will supply her with a baby, standing in for her longed-for penis. In the first moment of the Lacanian Oedipal complex, we re-meet this girl as grown woman, fulfilled. She has finally received her long-expected compensation penis-baby, her All. Her child, in a stroke of genius, is born into a critical lack, both hers and his own. In that sense, the child is experienced as the mother's phallus, i.e., her object of desire, resurrecting the illusion of being whole.

The child is born lacking in abilities to survive. The only thing that can compensate for his lack and ensure his safety is his mother's desire. But the lack of *this* infant, the Lacanian one, is oblivious of sex and gender. *All* infants lack. Their lack is inherent, organ-free and tied up with primal helplessness. The ticket to survival is given in an Imaginary reunion with mother and her body, close and inseparable as can be. It is here that we meet the first meaning of the Lacanian credo – *desire is a desire for the other's desire.* By embodying the ultimate object of her desire, the infant ensures mother's devotion and ongoing presence. Offering the perfection found in his mirror image, the child presents this ideal ego as *being* the mother's longed-for phallus (Lacan 1957–1958).

Now, notice the implicit paradox here: if the child is *impersonating* mother's object of desire, it means that he is aware that she has another object who is *not* himself. This is the sense in which Lacan claims that the father is always apparent in the child's primordial consciousness. Yet, in the Imaginary, the child can ignore differences and *collapse* into himself the other obscurely known object of mother's desire. Rare flashes that acknowledge mother's occasional absences resonate the 'unknown known' of her additional desire and drive the creation of the child's first primitive signifier of mother's desire: an unknown X marked by phi (φ).

In the second moment of the Oedipal phase, for development to occur, the child must be ousted from his position of *being* mother's sole object of desire. This happens when the child becomes cognizant of a prohibiting, punishing father. The child encounters this father only if he is given in mother's discourse. If the mother does not desire a father who claims her, the child will never encounter him. The mother's absences were there since birth, of course, but only Oedipal maturation brings the child to perceive and ascribe them to the painful existence of some other object of desire. Her absence *signifies* that she has an additional object of desire; where else would she go? In the Lacanian scheme of things, mother's absence is replaced with the positivity of an existing signifier that is associated with the unknown cause of her absence. If φ is the cause of mother's absence, S' signifies it as an Imaginary object. S' will then develop further (by a process of repression), becoming S1, namely, the-name-of-the-father.

The mother's progressively recognized absences are attributed by Freud to a prohibiting father who forbids endless jouissance between mother and child. But for Lacan, this Imaginary father and the threat of castration are not the crux of the matter; it is not they who set in motion the wheels of maturation. Development is not about organs, incest and fantasies of copulation, but rather about *desire*. The crucial moment here is when the child recognizes father as the object of mother's desire. If mother desires father, he must have something that makes him superior to the child, something that makes him more than an additional Imaginary being. This 'something' is given in the father's *Symbolic* nature.

The father here must represent a lawfulness that allows the mother-child dyad yet, at the same time, limits and exceeds it. He must both *represent* and be subject to this law. In this capacity, he need not be Imaginary or Real. He must be only Symbolic, which is why Lacan refers to him as 'the-**name**-of-the-father'. The physical father (i.e., the father in the bedroom) is superfluous in development. He need not exist at all. The necessary element is that the mother has desires additional to the desire for her child. These desires mark her as belonging to an order external to the one she inhabits with her child and this, in turn, triggers the child's wish to belong in that order herself. The Oedipal mother must be a Symbolic being, a being who is part of a social and cultural order and who desires her identity and satisfaction within it. In that sense, for the child to encounter lawfulness as something that exceeds the Imaginary, it is more than enough to encounter mother's 'other' desires; her will to get back to her job, to continue her Yoga classes or to read a book. Her desire must contain the wish to limit jouissance with her child and engage in other pleasures, needs and satisfactions.

What the mother desires in the father is the lawfulness of the Symbolic order. The grasp of this transforms the child's existential question from 'to be or not to be?' (the maternal phallus) into 'to have or not to have (it)?' *Here is the second meaning of the credo 'desire is a desire for the other's desire'.* Knowing who *has* it, the child now tries to figure out how he might obtain it. If mother's desire lies in the Symbolic, he will own it in the psychoanalytic way of owning: He will identify with the name-of-the-father, with his (m)other's Other.

In the third moment of the Oedipal drama the father is recognized as 'having it'. This constitutes him as the ego's ideal and drives the child to identify with him.[3] Effectually, this identification marks the entry of the first Symbolic element into the child's psyche – the name-of-the-father. Thus, the child enters the Symbolic order and becomes a subject in the world of language, law and desire. His horizons and desires expand and will heretofore be expressed in the love of ideas, culture and society – mostly in the medium of language. This transition from object of desire to desiring subject displays itself in the moment the child departs mother's lap and is no longer fed and perpetually coddled by her. Instead, he runs eagerly and ambitiously into the world and returns to mother with his 'conquests' in the Symbolic: a drawing from kindergarten, a puzzle completed or a letter written. He still aims at receiving her attention and love, but the realization of this desire is no longer determined by being her perfect object. Instead, he can be a knight of the Symbolic, owning and supplying mother with objects that elicit her pride. The child continues to experientially master mother's desire (by owning its object), without *being* that object. Being an object is now recognized as entailing the dangers of being obliterated and lost in the desiring subject.

With the identification of the name-of-the-father as the ego's ideal, the Oedipal complex is resolved. The consequences of this in terms of Symbolic functions are captured in the notion of the *paternal metaphor*, where linguistic workings are brought to the fore: "The function of the father in the Oedipus complex is to be a signifier substituted for the … first signifier introduced into symbolization, the maternal signifier" (Lacan 1957–1958, p.125). The name-of-the-father acts in the linguistic logic of metaphor to both assert and disconnect from the primitive desire of the mother. This sequence of repressions appears in Figure 3.1, where the horizontal lines represent repression and the timeline is from bottom to top (S1 is latest):

$$\frac{\dfrac{S1}{S'}}{x = \varphi}$$

Figure 3.1 The Oedipal process

This process of metaphorization is effectively the process of **primal repression** that ends the Oedipal complex and creates the Lacanian unconscious. In Figure 3.1, the upper bar represents the paternal metaphor as demarcating conscious and unconscious processes (respectively, identification with the father and desire of, or for, the mother). Here, the material of the unconscious is not body-based drives. Rather, it is alienated desire in the form of a primitive signifier (S'). That is why Lacan describes *the unconscious as being structured like a language.* It is comprised of signifiers.

The post-Oedipal child has transformed from object to desiring, speaking subject. Through language, she represents herself to others, makes choices and bears responsibility, creates meanings and models of reality. The Symbolic creates a realm of thirdness

(Lacan 1975), where thought develops, while Imaginary aggressivity is negotiated in beneficial spaces of social contracts. But these developments come at a price, and we can see here why the moment of the I's emergence is also the moment of its decline. For Lacan, every step forward entails a loss. The mother as Thing is lost to the signifier. The I's primary desire is lost and alienated. Hereon, the subject seeks the (maternal) object of her desire in the (paternal) Symbolic realm of law and language. She will represent herself and her desire by gliding along chains of signifiers, but as she moves forward, the subject also moves away from her original desire of mother and their mutual immersion in the jouissance of the Real.

3.3 Jouissance, lack and desire

Lacan calls a number of elements in the formation of the subject 'das Ding' (the Thing), one of which is the un-representable union with the primal mother. Oedipal alienation creates das Ding as an absolute externality that always conditions subjecthood. The 'I' is thrust forth from within the Thing, in an antagonistic movement, as an act of resistance to obliteration in mother's desire: "The 'I' denounces, rather than announces itself" (Lacan 1959–1960, p.56). When repressing (denouncing) 'desir de la mère' (simultaneously desire of and to the mother), the child departs das Ding and exits the realm of the Real, the realm of primal, submerged jouissance.

Simply stated, the ability to exist as differentiated subject is given in the inner ability – and unconscious consent – to replace jouissance with desire, to replace an unimagined fullness with lack. The Lacanian castration achieved in the Oedipal complex means that "jouissance has to be refused in order to be attained on the inverse scale of the Law of desire" (Lacan 1967, p.700). Hereon, **desire serves as a defense against jouissance**: It introduces a limit to the person's lustful self-erasure as an individual. In the dialectic tension that exists between jouissance and the subject (of lack, of desire) the sentence 'See Naples and die' can be understood not only as saying that there is nothing left to be seen in life after seeing Naples, but also as indicating that the experience of the city's beauty is too extreme and formidable to be experienced.

Leaving the subject in this Real(m) of experience is equivalent to her Symbolic death.

When the child recognizes that she is not mother's sole desire, she renounces her own perfection, her ideal ego, acknowledging that she is a lacking being. It is a strange and uniquely human characteristic that lack can be experienced as something positive. Lack of food is experienced as 'having an appetite', lack of achievement is experienced as 'having ambition and motivation'. Curiously (or not) having all one wants corresponds dangerously with depression (lack of desire) and a sad lack of motivation. This might be the root of the wise proverb: beware of having your dreams come true. Subjecthood is rooted in a lack.

Stated as abstract logic, lack drives signification (from maternal absence to φ and then S') which, in turn, creates further lack. For Lacan, the symbol implies 'the killing of the thing'. The 'Thing' represents that which is radically extraneous to the Symbolic, the 'beyond-of-the-signified', the un-representable; it marks the limits of meaning. In Lacan's words, "The thing is characterized by the fact that it is impossible to imagine" (Lacan 1959–1960, p.125). In other words, the Thing is Real, and in that sense, by killing it, "language forms a hole in the Real" (Lacan 1975–1976). The mother is not lost only because she comes and goes (as an Imaginary being). She is lost before that, with the severance of the (Real) umbilical cord, and again through the process of symbolization: "substituting its symbol for her has absented her ... orient-[ing] the life of the subject into a quest for redefining what was lost" (Ibid, p. 56). This resonates Freud's articulation of the futile, yet persistent, search for the lost object, never to be re-found. Entering the Symbolic, the subject enters a world in which his cravings will never be wholly satisfied. In that sense, *desire itself involves the pain of jouissance*: "What we find at the basis of ... desire is masochism ..." (Lacan 1957–1958) and: "The subject does not simply satisfy desire, he enjoys desiring (*jouit de désirer*) and this is an essential dimension of his *jouissance*" (Ibid, p.229).

Becoming a linguistic, Symbolic being, the subject sacrifices the possibility of ever re-finding the lost Thing. But here we find a Borromean link between the Real and the Symbolic: Language never remains purely Symbolic. It has an effect in the Real by creating a hole in it. Everything we say leaves something missing, unsaid, a remnant lost to the Real. But this is a very productive process: It keeps us talking, producing chains of signifiers, writing, creating poetry and science. It is in this realm that we find our satisfactions. We aspire, we achieve, we create. We enjoy our aspirations and the creativity they give rise to. We both enjoy and suffer the fact that we have no ultimate satisfactions. This keeps us always lacking, always wanting something more, always alive.

3.4 Castration, need and demand

Freud (1923) situated the discovery of sexual difference in the phallic stage. The child's world then divides between those who do and those who don't have it – the penis. The disappointed girl develops penis envy and, as described, hopes in time to receive her penis-baby. The little boy, seeing, penis-less girls and having already lost experienced body-parts (the mother's breast and the stool), fears castration as a concrete possibility, a punishment for his incestuous desires. In order to secure his physical integrity, he renounces his erotic attachments. As Lacan sees it, these Freudian dramas are wholly Imaginary. For him, castration is not about the penis, but rather about the paternal signifier. When this signifier enters the psychic economy, the child undergoes castration as a **two-tiered affair that involves separation from mother and alienation in language**. It is here that the positivity of jouissance transforms into the negativity of desire. All subjects, regardless of genital differences, undergo castration.

While Freudian castration centers on the penis, Lacanian castration involves the *signifier* (recall that the ϕ (phallus) is a signifier, a presence signifying absence). This shift from organ to sign is at the heart of Lacan's deconstructive reading of Freud and his re-definition of the body's functions in the constitution of mind and psychic structure. Development is dissociated from anatomy and predicated, instead, on the other. It is driven by desire towards this other and towards a sense of identity that cannot be achieved without him. The other is what tempted the child to divorce her authentic body experiencing, and adopt her mirror image as ego. In effect, the perceptual-cognitive-emotional process in which the infant discovers herself in external reality does not even require real mirrors. The mother, for example, can serve this function of the mirror just as well.

Symbolic developments, through the splitting effect of language, repeat and elaborate the alienating effect created by the primary, Imaginary, visual representation of self. The word not only kills the Thing, but also irrevocably tears the child from her animal existence, blurring and distorting her primal, physical being. From now on, all needs and desires are mediated by the forms and givens of the Symbolic order. Language does not arise from the individual, it is always there, in the world, outside. When it reaches the infant, she is initiated as subject into human existence, but she is also traumatized by it.

In order to satisfy needs, the child must express them in language, in the form of a *demand*. Demand, in that sense, is the mediated, Symbolic form of need. Representation creates an alienating distance between the subject and his needs, between needs and their representation. For Lacan, communication is alienating from the very beginning of life. When the infant cries out, the mother immediately interprets the cry in Symbolic terms. Holding her crying baby, walking to and fro, she tries to figure out what the infant wants, speaking to herself and to him: "You must be hungry, or cold ... your stomach aches again, you are probably tired and need to go to sleep ...". The mother's discourse regarding the source of the infant's distress *supplies him with possible categories of both distress and comfort*. According to *her* categories of thought and understanding, the child learns about what it is possible to want and wish for (in Symbolic terms). He also quickly learns where to expect comfort and which requests are likely to be met (or ignored). He learns to need what he can formulate and what he may expect to receive from the other and this is the additional distortion of need, added on to the translation of sensation to language. For example, the child may learn that he receives more sympathy when he says that he is tired than when he says he is afraid. It is small wonder that the subject is fatally restless. The impossibility of satisfaction resides in the innate distortion of need in symbolization and in the context of the other's desire.

Now, the mother's sympathy and responsiveness not only satisfy the original need: they also indicate her love. The mother may give her food offhandedly or with pleasure. She may put her child to bed impatiently or go with him gently into darkness when parting at night. It is in this way that the satisfaction of need comes to be associated with the infant's experience of his mother's desire for him. For Lacan (1967, pp.575–84), desire is what remains when need is subtracted from demand. In that sense, demand is for desire, for love. What the child receives is always both less and more than what he needs.

Deformation and alienation encompass every aspect of psychic life. Since language and signification precede the subject, he must bend his shape to accommodate himself to their pre-given, arbitrary forms. The purview of Symbolic hold extends to bodily functions. For example, jouissance initially inhabits the whole surface of the body; then it is evacuated to the openings of the body, creating the erotogenic zones. Freud thought that these areas are determined by the epigenetically programmed development of the drive, but Lacan saw them as vestiges of jouissance, centered (or even censored) by the dictates of the Other to socially acceptable zones.

3.5 The split subject

The Lacanian post-Oedipal subject is a tripartite entity across three orders that function in complex synchronizations. In the Symbolic order, the subject is split between conscious and unconscious domains created by the signifier and the law, language and culture, social roles, and norms. In the Imaginary, he exists as 'ego', namely, as a conscious self who is engaged in relations with specific, significant, *specular* others. The subject as *organism* exists in the Real, which is that part of experience that evades all representation, both Imaginary and Symbolic. Lacan sees subject and organism as existing on different sides of an unbridgeable divide, leaving the subject split and without a firm identity.

The general structure of the subject as split and spanning the various orders is given in Lacan's Schema L (Lacan 1954–1955, p.243) in more or less the following form:

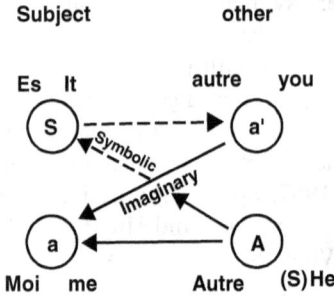

Figure 3.2 The basic Schema L

In this diagram, we can see that the orders of the Symbolic and the Imaginary are presented as relationships between a particular manifestation of the subject and a particular manifestation of the other. Thus, the Symbolic order is presented as spanning the space between the big Other (A/(S)He) and the subject of the Unconscious (Es/It), depicting the close bond that exists between the subject's unconscious and the discourse of the Other. In a similar manner, the Imaginary is seen here as the space between the first person 'me' (ego) and the second person 'you', presented as the generalization of the specular other. The crossing of the axes in the middle of the Schema should be thought of not only as a 'blocking' and a 'crossing', but also as the knotting convolution of the orders in the Borromean diagram (Figure 2.1).

Schema L can be used to depict a special form of 'thick' communication, such as in psychoanalytic communication. By distinction, thin communication, news broadcasts for example, encompass only partial dimensions of communication. They usually assume an *intentionality* in singular form and thus largely limit themselves to conscious processes (me and you). They also construe communication as a process in which a message is sent by *one* agent (the sender) to another (the addressee). In psychoanalytic treatment we indeed have a person with a conscious intentionality speaking. But we never assume that he is the *sole* creator of his message. We always assume an additional intentionality that is implicated in speech and goes beyond the conscious purpose. The signifiers produced by the 'me' create the conscious account of who this 'me' is. And yet, this chain of signifiers is always, in different ways, influenced by the primal, repressed signifiers of the unconscious. The unconscious has a separate agency ('Es' in Schema L), throwing signifiers of *its* choice into the metonymic chain in ways that may radically change their meanings. In this sense, there are always (at least) two agencies in the context of analytic speech. The 'me' is roughly equivalent to the grammatical first person appearing in a sentence like 'I want to make love to my girlfriend'. The 'Es' is the subject of enunciation. In our illustrative sentence, Es can totally change the meaning of the sentence, for example, by inserting the word 'sister' instead of 'girlfriend'.

For Lacan, the unconscious is not only an object of interpretation. Part of its linguistic character is created when it acts as an agency that interprets. Any message that we receive from ourselves or from others is given in chains of signifiers and significations that activate our unconscious and create additional chains, according to the principles of metaphor and metonymy. In that sense, the Lacanian unconscious is always productive, creating formations that the subject is unaware of, a kind of 'knowledge without a subject'. Where dream materials, associations or slips are enunciated, the subject bumps into this knowledge and encounters deeper layers of repressed desires. In that sense, "in human speech the sender is always a receiver at the same time" (Lacan 1955–1956, p.24).

Vaguely aware of this unknown knowledge, the neurotic is perpetually disturbed by the two questions that were central in instating the primal repression: 'Who am I?' and 'What does the other want'? These questions are inextricably inter-related, with the other's desire providing the answer to the question of who I am or may be. For Lacan, identity is forever given in the form of a question, with an other supplying the answer, be he an 'internal' or 'external' other. Lacan believes that this pattern should be overcome in analysis, allowing the subject to cease shaping desire in accordance with the other's desire. The analysand is of course addressing the analyst but, at the same time, he also sends a message from his unconscious to his conscious self. The analyst is

expected to position herself as Other in order to allow interpretation to return to the analysand with its unconscious dimension:

> If one wants to position the analyst within this schema of the
> subject's speech, one can say that he is somewhere in A. At least
> he should be. If he enters into the coupling of the resistance,
> which is just what he is taught not to do, then he speaks from *a'*
> and he will see himself in the subject.
>
> (Lacan 1955–1956, pp.161–2)

He will then be inserting his own conscious messages, obstructing
the unconscious dimension. Only by refraining from acting as *a'*
will the analyst allow "the sender [to] receive[s] his own message
from the receiver in an inverted form" (Lacan 1967, p.30).

These readings of Schema L underline the weaving of the orders
with the various relations of subject and other. The Schema also
depicts the manner in which the subject is split *intra-subjectively.*
Lacan (1967, p.459) says that the subject "… is stretched over the
four corners of the schema". This means that the subject is always
multiform, with an unconscious Es, an unconscious *a'*, a conscious
moi and a partly-conscious A. In this reading of Schema L, *a'*
functions as an alter-ego in the Imaginary, with which the subject
is always entangled and which expresses his narcissistic infatuation
and aggressivity. Finally, he holds *within* him or herself a partly-
conscious big Other, an A who preceded him, and who he has
internalized as a part of himself. Here, the Symbolic axis conveys the
dialectic between the big Other and its unconscious internalization.

What sustains across all interpretations of Schema L is the decen-
tering of the subject, because each corner of the schema assumes a
different subject positioning. Speech evokes different intentionalities
irrespective of context, and some always remain unaccounted for.
For example, when I speak to my boss, two intentionalities are
immediately present: Me (moi) and my boss (*a'*). In addition, there is
also my child self, or perhaps a vulnerable sexual being (Es), speaking to my father or my mother, or perhaps to an internalized institution (A). Then again, the first person (moi) may speak from an
identification with A, thus collapsing the first and the third persons.
Even in this reduced situation, the message still activates both the

Imaginary self (*a'*) and various configurations of the unconscious, such as possible resistances to authority (Es).

There are many ways in which schema L may be applied and interpreted, including some in which the directionality of the arrows traverses the various inter- and intra-subjective relations among parts of the self and the other. *This means that the subject is in constant flux, always influenced and recreated by the signifiers he hears and utters.* And yet, what is consistently not represented in the schema L is the order of the Real. This is no coincidence and has to do with the evolution of Lacan's thought. Schema L served as a constant point of reference in the 1950s, when Lacan was figuring out the way in which awareness of the Symbolic may free the subject from Imaginary shackles. In the late 1960s, Lacan dedicated increasingly more thought to the Real and the ways its effects may be utilized in psychoanalysis, which made him move from schematic diagrams to topological diagrams. To account for these developments, we offer here a revised diagram of Schema L that integrates the Real into the portrayal of the decentered subject and his inevitable ties with o\Others. This addition will indicate that in any subject position – me, I, Other or other – the decentered subject is tied up with his material organism.

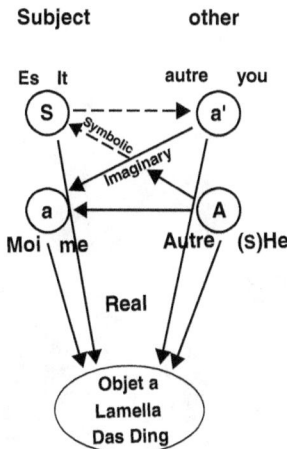

Figure 3.3 The extended Schema L

The extended Schema L contributes to our understanding of the relationship between the orders in a number of ways. First, as we stated repeatedly, the Real indicates the many gaps in both of the other orders, represented by the crossings it creates in both the Imaginary and the Symbolic. Second, by showing the Real to inhabit a whole dimensionality, we convey the idea that the bulk of mental life always escapes representation. Since our claim to knowledge is based on representation, the diagram conveys the limits of knowing. Third, the diagram connects the subject to determinants that elucidate different aspects of the Real: Das Ding, the body, lamella and the *objet a*. As we will see in the next chapters, signifiers affect the Real of the subject in fateful ways that are relevant to both sexuation and the therapeutic endeavor.

Notes

1 Space doesn't allow us to discuss the intricate relations of temporal and logical time.
2 Other psychoanalytic languages describe this as *symbiosis*.
3 "It is in so far as he intervenes at the third moment as the one who, for his part, has it, that he is interiorized as ego-ideal in the subject ... at that very moment the Oedipus complex dissolves" (Lacan 1957–1958, p.139).

Chapter 4

The Fundamental Fantasy

The fundamental fantasy is formed at the moment of the 'big bang' in the constitution of the Lacanian subject, the moment the name-of-the-father enters the child's psychic economy. It is then that the child transforms from object of desire to desiring subject and leaves behind the Thing and the realm of jouissance. The paternal metaphor that replaces the signifier of maternal desire creates the unconscious and, with it, the multi-dimensional representations of triadic space. This leads to the differentiation of self from other.

And yet, at the very base of his newly created unconscious, the child begins to harbor an unconscious fantasy of reunion, a longing for what he had just now renounced, a yearning that will haunt him all his life: to return to the symbiotic, endless perfection of jouissance he had found in the undifferentiated matrix with mother. This is the fundamental fantasy: *it depicts our particular and consistent ways of dealing with loss, of undoing and denying castration, differentiation and lack.* The origin of the fantasy is similar for all, but the shape it takes is totally individual, nourished by the circumstances of one's family life.

4.1 Preliminary description

When the undifferentiated mother-child unit divides into its elements and forms two split and lacking subjects, the shattered primordial union emits an additional particle, a 'remainder': The *objet petit a* (also referred to as 'petit *a*', or '*a*'). The *objet petit a* is a particle of the Real that had escaped the paternal prohibition and now holds

DOI: 10.4324/9781003106883-4

the lost, limitless jouissance of undifferentiated existence. It represents what both mother and child had lost and what, if retrieved, might make them whole again.

The basic definition of the fundamental fantasy involves the divided subject's relation to *objet a*. Lacan's shorthand way of expressing the basic fantasy is given in a matheme[1] of three signifiers that represent the positioning of its elements.

$$\mathcal{S} \lozenge a$$

Figure 4.1 Matheme of fantasy structure

Here, $\mathcal{S}$ is the split subject, *a* is the *objet petit a* and $\lozenge$ represents the various possible ways in which the subject may position himself in relation to *objet a*, namely, the exclusive desire of the other and its related jouissance. Since desire is always for the other's desire and the *objet a* holds this desire in its most intensive primordial guise, *a* becomes the *object-cause of the subject's desire*. The subject's relation to the *objet a* is effectively his relation to, and contact with, the Real. It grants him the dimension of being in raw and authentic experience. Forming the core of the unconscious, the fundamental fantasy is static and serves as the unconscious representation of what may undo the child's loss of unity with his (m)Other. It grants a fixed form to the craving for an intense meeting of desires that will resonate the forever-lost jouissance, the unmediated totality that had characterized early, pre-Symbolic life. Throughout his life the subject will fluctuate between the intense unconscious desire to re-unite with *objet a* (as stand-in for the Thing) and the desire to keep his distance from it, and thus protect his status as Symbolic subject. This fluctuation, like the conflict it expresses, will never resolve and thus perpetuate the subject's incessant psychic motion. The *objet a*, as an object of lack (and lack of the object) realizes the Lacanian maxim: No psychic motion is possible without lack.

4.2 Fantasy and desire

The Lacanian subject 'wants' in the sense of the inherent interconnectivity between will and lack. In accordance with his anti-essentialist stance, Lacan offers here a prime theoretical achievement: a formulation of human motivation that is divorced from the body. Instead, he construes both Eros and the death drive as weaving bodily sensation with semiotic reasoning. This is encapsulated in the notion of the fundamental fantasy.

The Lacanian Eros is borne of separation from the maternal body. It is neither innate nor bodily given. It is primitively relational and uncompromisingly tied up with an unattainable externality: "the true nature of the Trieb ... is not simply instinct, ... [it] has a relationship to das Ding as such ..." (Lacan 1959–1960, p.123). The subject will never re-appropriate the Thing or its remainder, the *objet a*. Indeed, if she did, it would involve the paradox of undoing the very act that had brought her into existence, namely, differentiation from the other. In that sense, *the drive towards objet a* is a death drive, *marking the meltdown of subjectivity*. It promises the intensity of jouissance in primitive form, but entails the complete destruction of self and other in a core reunion. This is a terrifying yet alluring site of singularity, the site of das Ding, which Lacan called the 'core of *destrudo*' (Ibid, p.194).

For Lacan, this is "the essential affinity of every drive with the zone of death" and what reconciles "the two sides of the drive which, at one and the same time, makes present sexuality in the unconscious and represents, in its essence, death" (Ibid, p.73). What stands between the alluring 'core of destrudo' and the subject is the (re-defined) pleasure principle, which governs the search for the object and imposes the detours that maintain the subject's distance from it.

The search for the object encounters in its path a series of satisfactions, leading "... the subject from signifier to signifier, generating as many signifiers as are required to maintain at as low a level as possible the tension that regulates the whole functioning of the psychic apparatus" (Ibid, p.119). Enjoyment never exceeds a certain level of excitation: "... The point is: enjoyment is our barrier from jouissance and therefore from aggressivity and narcissism, from merger, from the inevitable destruction in das Ding – the object of jouissance. Therefore, the superego commands: ENJOY!" (Ibid, p.323) and ensures that the subject stays within the limits of enjoyment and measured satisfactions, without giving in to the tempting intensities of jouissance. This limiting of jouissance is the prime function of the Lacanian pleasure principle. What holds jouissance at bay is desire.[2]

We can see here one of Lacan's recurring subversive moves: using Freud's terminology with a totally different set of meanings. Whereas Freud's drive is innate, Lacan's drive is born from the subject's search for what he had lost when re-losing his primal connection with the mother. Freud's object is defined by the drive. Lacan's object predates the subject and his loss creates desire. The un-monitored movement towards primal jouissance and symbiotic relation with the other is effectively the *death drive*. Desire will always keep jouissance at bay. Like Freud, Lacan's life force is an offshoot of the death drive.

How does this fantasy – this nostalgic, persistent craving for merger and return to the womb – manifest experientially? Consider, for example, turning off the alarm clock and the phone, and deciding not to get out of bed. We forgo the duties that mark our positioning as subjects of a social order and disappear under the covers, wanting nothing but to sleep. We experience ourselves at such a moment as giving way to a luring gravity that knows no lack. We settle under the covers and allow ourselves to drift into sleep. A similar experiential state might be created during a late-night binge on ice-cream and a series we have already seen. Eating ice-cream in bed, knowing that we are safe from critical gazes, we revel in having it all, in needing nothing but our ice-cream and Netflix. What usually puts a stop to such binges of jouissance is *anxiety*. At some point we will experience a shock of apprehension, fear that we won't get up the next morning to deliver our important presentation, that we are endangering our conceptions of health.

What actually happens in the situations described above is that we experience 'a lack of a lack' and the danger of forgoing our existence as desiring (Symbolic) subjects. Much as we crave the *objet a*, the Real jouissance of primal merger, we also hold deep knowledge that we came into existence as subjects by differentiating from this very merger. Much as we miss it, we refuse returning to the status of being the exclusive object of the other's desire and jouissance. We crave it, but we know it holds our demise.

Understanding this, we recognize the fundamental fantasy's paradoxical double function. On the one hand, the fantasy allows the illusion of re-attaining our lost primordial union, touching upon what otherwise is utterly beyond reach. On the other hand, the fantasy employs several measures that serve as a defense against achieving this craved-for merger.

4.3 Imaginary and Symbolic effects

The fundamental fantasy grants Imaginary dimensions to *objet a* as the object-cause of desire. The many *consciously experienced* objects of our desire are Imaginary guises for the thing that we imagine will ignite the other's desire. We imagine that 'having' this object will grant us pure, ecstatic and unmediated pleasure. This falls in with the metonymic character of desire, which incessantly shifts among signifiers. All the displacements of *objet a* retain certain phantasmatic features which, when encountered in a potential object, ensure that we desire it. Thus, the cause of the subject's desire becomes its object, or rather, a whole series of objects.

The subject may imagine that he will be totally and permanently satisfied if only he came to own a certain car, achieve a certain weight, buy a certain perfume, find a certain partner, obtain a university degree. *This* particular thing will make him whole, totally, and exclusively desired by the other. Unfailingly, these Imaginary semblances fall away and reveal their true nature as guises once we possess them. Once we reach the desired weight, we realize we will be perfect, happy and desirable only when we get our nose fixed. Once we have our bachelor's degree, we realize it was a master's that we were aiming for. Once we find the perfect partner, we inevitably find him disappointing. And yet, this metonymic movement among Imaginary and Symbolic objects is the productive factor of desire. It keeps us on the move, always searching for new objects, always revealing new horizons from the apex we had formerly achieved. It keeps us desiring, aspiring and alive, enjoying satisfactions along the way and, hopefully, learning to enjoy the way itself.

The fantasy also employs the Imaginary by involving ourselves in a *scene* that positions us in relation to the desire of the other.

For example, the fantasy of the child who is being beaten (as in Freud 1919) positions the subject in relation to the other's desire to punish. The scene is usually rigid, almost meticulously cere-monious. Why the fixed character? Because already, by definition, the scene holds for us, alongside its temptations, an uncanny fear of (un)known death, given in vague bodily memories of jouis-sance. Thus, when we fantasize, say, the perfect hug, any tiny change of detail may destroy it. If the hug lasts too long, if it is a bit too lax or tight, this will somehow acquire an additional dimension (say sweatiness), to which we will react with excessive repulsion or even fear. It is not that we are so ticklish in the pragmatics of our jouissance. It is rather that moving any element in the well-orchestrated scene reveals what it hides – our potential death. We can see here how death, desire and jouissance are for-ever tied up in intricate ways, how we always simultaneously crave life and death. The rigidity of the fantasy allows it to 'hide' the dynamic, uncanny pull to what lies behind it. Therefore, fantasies may be extremely satisfying, but their realization can be terribly disappointing.

The fantasy serves an additional purpose by providing a *stable defense* against the necessary fact of castration, i.e., the awareness of lack in both self *and other*. The *objet a* potentially renders both self and other whole and it is here that we begin discussing the pertinence (and folly) of perceiving the Other as whole. As said before, we live in accordance with the Other's laws, rules and structures. To exist with some peace of mind, we need to trust this Other, to have faith in his determination of ourselves and our lives. As Horkheimer has shown (1972), many people imagine that social structures are a *given*, dictated by nature, God, or some other metaphysical, uncontestable entity that serves as the guar-antee for stability and sense in our lives. Knowing that the Other *lacks* may lead us to lose our sense of security in the way things are. Of course, this may also be of benefit, depending on the sub-ject's reaction to the fact that 'there is no Other of the Other', meaning that the Other is perhaps, like in Joan Osborne's song, *One of Us*, "… just a slob like one of us / just a stranger on the bus / trying to make his way home". Grasping this is the equiva-lent of experiencing and re-experiencing the Nietzschean moment when God is pronounced dead and the world is thrown into disarray. In that sense, the fantasy allows us to preserve the Big Other as Big; as a parent who may take care of us, protect and keep us from being orphaned.

Viewed with a larger perspective, the fantasy's rigid character grants us *consistency* as subjects of desire, metonymically gliding in a world of desires. *It grants a formal frame on the modes and motions of our desire.* To repeat, there is no objective world in the Lacanian universe, only ways of construing it according to relevant parameters which, for the subject, are first and foremost his desire and jouissance. This throws into relief the pertinence of the fantasy. Shaping our desire is effectually shaping the way we construe ourselves and our world. This means that the fantasy determines our perception of reality and our horizons as subjects. It keeps us moving in certain directions, looking for certain things, making us blind to others.

4.4 Some clinical effects

As long as the fantasy fulfills its function of granting us stability, we can easily point out its productive force. On a negative track, we can identify two patterns – a rigid and obsessive fixation on a specific manifestation of *objet a* or, alternatively, a repetitive cycle that doesn't produce creativity. Instead, it evokes obstinate repetitions across various objects that, even when they change, achieve little in our patterns of satisfaction. Lacan emphasizes this aspect of the fantasy, tying up repetition compulsion with death. This implies endless, demonic-like repetition of what we see, do and seek, even when these repetitions grant no satisfaction or happiness. In this situation, jouissance reduces to masochistic and sadistic practices.

These rigid repetitions are easily identified in daily life. Take, for example, the Apple-freak who gets up at 3am to stand in an endless queue for a new gadget. His house is already full of unused instruments that fired his imagination when first announced, but then their Imaginary guise was revealed and they became worthless or even, at times, abject. He is oblivious of the way his expenses might affect his family budget and may not be aware of whose sleep he disturbs at 3am. An obsessive version of this may manifest in FOMO[3] phenomena, keeping people exhausted and on the run, not noticing what they miss by not remaining in one place, with one person. In a romantic vein, this may present as the woman who waits for the perfect man and loses herself in repetitive rumination, blind to the virtues of those around her; or in the syndromes of Don Juan or femme fatale that keep people compulsively moving from one partner to the next.

In Lacan's eyes, there is not much that is uplifting in the fantasy's effects. If for Freud 'anatomy is destiny', for Lacan 'fantasy is destiny', because its derivatives determine the ways subjects live their lives. Of course, one needs a measure of anchoring and consistency, but the fantasy forecloses the dissemination of desire and its possibilities and may trap the subject in repetitive rigid obsessions.

And yet, the baby must not be thrown out with the bath water: The fantasy may play an important part in our love life in two ways. Firstly, the fantasy creates desire, because we see the world in accordance with its patterns. It makes us chose our partners and brings us to enjoy them. Without it, we may not have looked at people or noticed them. Moreover, it is a question if any love relation can exist without a quota of fantasy-driven idealization. Lacan discusses this aspect of *objet a* when he considers *courtly love* as a version of idealizing that raises the beloved to the level of divinity. In a typical Lacanian paradox, idealization lays on a par with the 'Ding' as *objet a* and the beloved. This, of course, will necessarily lead to disappointment, but perhaps many of us would choose not to empty our life of ecstatic infatuations because, at times, the ride is worth the fall.

The contact with the Real is a true craving of the subject and grants her a form of *being* that is often more potent, exciting and stimulating than her usual existence in the bonds of social conventions and Symbolic restrictions. Lacan (1967, pp.530–7) believed that every subject's fundamental fantasy has a unique and personal set of features that allow her to sustain herself in the face of fading desire. In the Symbolic she is, in a sense, an 'everyman'. The fantasy puts her in touch with the Real, where she experiences her invigorating singularity. Indeed, the subject may often find herself divided between Real and Symbolic motives: Why did she marry this exciting woman instead of a wealthy woman who would make her life easier? Why did she choose this charming man when her mother had always told her he would not make a good husband? The more we try to explain the choice, the further it strays from rational explanation, because the Real cannot be expressed or explained. It can only be experienced, among other things, in the expansion of the lover's self.

4.5 Fantasy and society

Capitalism offers a prime example of the way global social networks can enact a fundamental fantasy in obsessive, repetitive cycles. Fads, fashions and 'must-haves' clearly illustrate how *needs* (or *pseuo-needs*) may seize discourse across countries and nations. Its fantastic nature may be seen in the way most of us manage very well without once attaining it. The advertising system utterly relies on this structure. The advertised object is ordinarily presented by a man or woman who embody contemporary forms of perfection. Instantly we want it and imagine ourselves as happy and attractive 'owners' of it. Moreover, the dynamics of the fantasy is such that even if we own the fantasied object we still maintain a want of it.

Communal fantasies are not only wasteful but may also be dangerous. Consider Trump's slogan 'Make America Great Again'. It embodies more than naive nostalgia for Mayflower and the Wild West. Lurking between the signifiers is the 'pure' and 'whole' American. It conceals denial of historical injustices, alongside xenophobia and ideals of white supremacy. Constructing state or race on themes of a fundamental fantasy is dangerous; it draws its social and political strength from the illusion and force of the fantasy and may create despotic regimes through mergers of citizen and state.

The above examples provide us with a wonderful chance to examine the curiosity and trickiness of the Lacanian unconscious, that lies both within and without, linking 'external' realities to the 'discourse of the Other' within us. Take for example the fantasy of white supremacy. Any liberal will lay down his life denying he holds any belief of this kind, yet he might be surprised, or even uncomfortable, that his brain surgeon is African-American. A secular Jew will deny believing that Jews are a 'chosen people' and flaunt his acceptance of minorities. Yet, how many Israeli Jews would choose an Arab as neighbor? Are these forms of queasy preferences derivatives of a Freudian death drive? Or perhaps internalized social constructions? The decentered subject is spread over many levels and dimensions of existence. The subject is more caught up in her society's fundamental fantasy than she would like to admit.

4.6 Fantasy and the body

Before wrapping up the subject of the fundamental fantasy, we wish to discuss one additional context that relates to the body. In Seminar 11, Lacan (1963–1964) discusses the *objet a* in terms of the original 'cut' from the other, reiterating the moment of separation from the (m)other that gradually accumulates into self-differentiation. The *objet a* marks the distinction between the maternal body and the body of the subject, and the experienced dimensions of inside and outside integral to the subject's emergence: "In order to have a complete notion of this pre-specular totality ... [*objet a*], you have to consider these [maternal] envelopes as elements of the [subject's] body" (Lacan 1962–1963, p.106). The 'cut' will terminate the experience of a mother-infant common body, but as it occurs in that primordial, merged body, it will be experienced as occurring *within* it. "The cut ... if we have recognized ... [the] analogy between oral weaning and the weaning of birth, ... is inside the individual ... [W]here the cut is made between what is going to become the individual ... these envelopes which form part of himself ..." (Ibid, p.214). The fundamental cut is the separation at birth from the placenta which, in turn, may serve as the prototype of *objet a*. It is conjoined to the mother, but does not naturally belong to her body and develops only when she is pregnant in order to deliver nutrition to the fetus. When separating from the placenta, the infant undergoes division from its immersion in the nurturing formlessness of organic life. Separating the child from the non-differentiated organic body of the mother separates him from *himself*, effecting a division of the subject in the Real.

In a manner similar to that of the placenta, from the infant's point of view, the breast also becomes redundant after weaning. Initially the breast is the ultimate object of the child's survival and is experienced as part of his own body. For Winnicott (1969), optimal development occurs when the mother is ready to grant the child an omnipotent illusion of control. The child then experiences the breast as appearing upon his command, just like his own foot or hand would do. Only gradually, with maturation and non-traumatic frustration, the child discovers separateness. For Lacan, this separation is *inherently* traumatic, a cut, reiterating the caesura of birth.

In the Lacanian universe generally, the moments of separation – the Real division at birth, the Imaginary coupling of the imago and the Symbolic separation from (m)other – always and inevitably carry the traumatic character of a cut. They leave their mark on the body and create patterns of fantasy. The mother's breast creates the mouth as an erotic zone. The stool, which was a treasure during toilet training, becomes redundantly abject,[4] but leaves the anal zone eroticized. The images of these abject objects remain ready to use in fantasies and dreams, holding the vestiges of jouissance once belonging to them. Among the body parts that act as *objet a*, Lacan includes the eye and the voice. They too point to the Real and figure in fantasy life. As adults, we still experience jouissance with a loving gaze upon us, or a voice that comes to comfort us (as in guided meditation). These are the resonances of mother's gaze and voice. These 'cuts' are made at points of entry from and to the other, usually (but not necessarily) in the clearer openings of our porous bodies. Some coincide with Freud's 'erotogenic zones', where contact with an other holds the potential for both jouissance and abjection throughout life.

Much as we want to be seen, we will be anxious to feel that we are being *watched*. Much as we crave the voice of the other, we will be anxious to find it permanently in our mind. Human voices are always more for us than the information they convey. We will always retain a strange mixture of the abject and the divine in relation to erotogenic contact with the other because of its ability to resonate primary merger. We can never quite convey, unravel, and formulate these experiences of contact with the Real, but they are given in our fantasy and held by *objet a*.

Notes

1 This shorthand formation is called 'matheme' because it takes on some features of a mathematical formula without actually being one.
2 In Seminar 11 Lacan presents an alternative account of Eros, yet retains the same logic. Libido is represented here by an 'organ' of sorts – the lamella – which is a part of the body lost at birth. It marks the most profound lost object as Real. At birth we all lose simple, indestructible life-as-organ: "It is precisely what is subtracted from the living being by virtue of the fact that it is subject to the cycle of sexed reproduction" (Lacan 1963–1964, p.197). While being highly abstract, the lamella is also very concrete, a piece of meat, so to speak, as if libido has an organ for itself. Lacan writes: "the lamella is something extra-flat which moves like the amoeba. ...it is, like the amoeba in relation to sexed being, immortal – because it survives any division, any scissiparous intervention. And it can run around. This lamella, this organ, whose characteristic is not to exist, but which is nevertheless an organ ... is the libido" (Ibid, p.198). This energetic side of the Real is oblivious to sex and gender. It is neither masculine nor feminine, but the relation between the living subject and that which he loses by having to pass, for his reproduction, through the sexual cycle. In Seminar 11 it is this loss that all objects of desire come to represent. Despite the different terms and accounts, the essential point remains: the life force is borne of separation from the maternal body.
3 Fear Of Missing Out
4 'Abject' is the term coined by Julia Kristeva (1982) to refer to an object that arouses in the subject the need to reject it. The abject is associated with a degree of nausea, but we are always also drawn to it.

Chapter 5

The Clinical Structures

Lacanian diagnostics aligns with Lacan's persistent deconstruction of binaries and distances itself from claims about pathology and health. The Lacanian clinical structures are *consistent modes of subjectivity, predicated upon the relations between the desires of subject and Other.* Recall that modes of desire determine both identity and reality. Therefore, the subject's clinical structure is telling of his construal of self and world, his apperceptive and behavioral patterns and his ways of object relating. It is not particular symptoms that determine diagnosis, but rather a general way of living.

Subjectivity involves the dialectics of desire. It negotiates a fine balance between renouncing and maintaining primal jouissance as a phantasmatic possibility. Subjects differ in the ways they alternate between recognizing and denying castration, with its derivative differentiations and losses. The different clinical structures reflect some consistencies in the manner the subject does this. They hinge upon the particular mechanism that negates castration. The pervert *denies*, the neurotic represses and the psychotic *forecloses*. In that sense, the clinical structures reflect the subject's positioning in relation to the Other's desire. As such, diagnosis may act as a guide for clinical technique.

5.1 Neurosis

The developmental itinerary of the neurotic is the canonical one: the paternal metaphor properly constitutes her unconscious,

DOI: 10.4324/9781003106883-5

displacing maternal jouissance for the paternal signifier. This drives alienation and leads to misnaming the neurotic's desire. It creates the dominant feature of her makeup: she never quite knows what she wants. She represents her desire in chains of signifiers that formally and content-wise accord with Symbolic law, but she doesn't seem to gain any peace of mind. This movement is represented in Figure 5.1.

The diagram shows the paternal metaphor, where S1 represents the name-of-the-father. S1 is situated in the unconscious (in accordance with the repression of the Oedipal Complex) and holds under it, in deeper repression, the more primitive signifier of the mother's desire (which in various texts appears as S' or as φ). S1 functions as a *master signifier* in the Symbolic, ruling and ordering all other signifiers in accordance with the prohibition of incest. This is the cornerstone of social structure. The straight arrow along the signifiers (S2 ... Sn), represents desire's inauguration in the Symbolic order. The various signifiers mark the neurotic's representation of herself in the social world. She may be a family or community member, a friend, a colleague, a writer, a speaking being, etc.

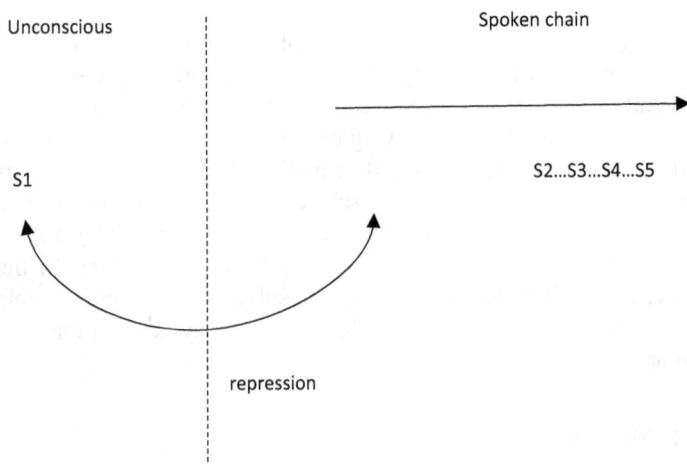

Figure 5.1 Neurotic signification

The rounded arrow represents a feature of the neurotic's existence that is both local and general. Locally, the meaning of her sentences, actions and narratives are worked out backwards, in après-coup fashion, when each signifier grants meaning to those that precede it. 'Garden path' sentences illustrate this property of speech. Their beginning leads you to understand a meaning that in the end transpires not to be the real meaning of the sentence. Take for example, the sentence 'I know the words to that song about the queen don't rhyme'. Until the final two words, the sentence is understood as being about someone who knows the words of a song about the queen. The final words 'don't rhyme' oblige us to rework the sentence's meaning: The speaker knows that the words of the song don't rhyme. Lacan generalizes this property, construing the neurotic subject as always given in the process of *becoming*, with the present perpetually recreating the past. This paradoxical extension of Freud's 'afterward' effect ('deferred action' in the Standard Edition) *grants the subject's structure a hermeneutic character*. This is what allows us to recreate the past via interpretation.

The neurotic constitutes her identity by identifying with an ideal of the ego and she is forever trying to live up to it. The two questions that determine her early development haunt her throughout life, yet the second question serves as an answer of the first: 'Who am I?' and 'What does the other want?' It may be 'I am she who wants to find a cure for cancer, because the world desires this' or 'I want a college degree, because it will make me desirable', etc. This may also take a negative form, adhering to the same logic: 'I will not be a doctor because this is what my mother desires of me'. Whether in positive or negative form, the neurotic trap is that, on the one hand, the subjection to the Other's desire feels oppressive and truncates one's own desire. On the other hand, the desire is for the other's desire. Moreover, obtaining the other's desire forever still holds the promise of regaining lost jouissance. Sadly, achieving this entails the end of existence as desiring subject. This can be formulated as the chronic struggle between the Lacanian life and death drives. In the throes of the fundamental fantasy, the neurotic subject finds ways in which she tries holding both ends of the stick, maintaining both the promise and possibility of jouissance *and* the lack and desire that sustain her as subject. The two modes of accomplishing this feat define Lacan's Hysteric and Obsessive.[1]

5.2 The Obsessive

The Obsessive responds to castration by denying its consequences and not acknowledging her lack. She pretends that she owns *objet a* and that the Other has nothing to do with it. In other words, the Obsessive poses as totally self-sufficient, and therefore cannot acknowledge or bear desire or differentiation. Given this need to petrify desire, the Obsessive's existential question concerns her very existence: 'Am I alive or dead?'

Lacan ties the Obsessive up with a mother who desired the father but was dissatisfied with their relations. She compensated by nurturing a special, favoring relationship with the child. This leaves margins for the child to continue maintaining his position as maternal phallus, her precious, desired object. Not wanting to surrender this jouissance-rewarding position, the Obsessive is deeply ambivalent regarding the paternal function. He repeatedly challenges it (this explains the obsessive characteristic of contrariness), yet he also desperately needs it in order not to lose himself in mother's desire. Finding himself eventually giving in to both mother's desire and the paternal law, the Obsessive feels enslaved and swamped by demand. To escape this deadlock, she may resort to the tactic of nullifying herself or the other. Since self and other are inextricable, the difference is not essential, but rather a difference in flavor, tone or emotional pattern.

The Obsessive nullifies herself, 'plays dead', so that Others can't really get anything out of her. She performs duties impeccably, but beneath her superficial compliance lies an adamant refusal to give anything of her desire. Referencing Hegel's master-slave dialectic (Hegel 1807; Lacan 1953–1954, p.97) Lacan describes this behavioral pattern: The slave (the Obsessive) had given up the struggle for mastery when faced with death. Yet, as he now knows his own mortality, he also knows his master's. Temporarily renouncing jouissance, the slave outwardly complies, and patiently awaits his master's death. This accounts for "the doubt and procrastination that are ... prime obsessive character traits" (Ibid, p.97). Trans-forming all desire into demand, the Obsessive's life is an endless rigorous adherence to rules and regulations. This transformation actually nullifies both self and Other, since usually the Obsessive lives by demands seemingly posed by the Other. And yet, by replacing desire with demand, the Obsessive paradoxically *sustains* himself as subject of desire because, in its 'underground' mode, his desire cannot be subjected to an Other. This is how the Obsessive hoards the precious, empty secret of his alienated, unsatisfied desire.

The Obsessive's stability is predicated on experiencing herself as complete. She therefore hates desire, as it always indicates lack. She prefers solitude or love for an unattainable object rather than real relationships. If she ventures to love someone, she will be extremely controlling. This may range from bossiness to forms of stalking and violent control. As the unconscious harbors desire, the Obsessive hates it. Accordingly, she is a poor candidate for either love or therapy.

5.3 The Hysteric

The Hysteric is more developed than his Obsessive colleague. He acknowledges lack but positions it wholly in the realm of the Other. He instates himself as the cause and object of the other's desire – his *objet a*, able to 'plug' the other's lack. In order to achieve this, the Hysteric must closely observe this other, figuring out and impersonating whatever (s)he desires. This makes the Hysteric an artist of temptation, with particular sensitivities, identification with the other and characteristic suggestiveness. Lacan sums this up with the idea that the Hysteric never quite knows whether (s)he is a man or a woman.

The Hysteric's plight creates a paradox: Since his whole being concerns the ability to mend the Other's lack, he must maintain this lack in order to exist. He then engages in impersonating everybody's *objet a* and risks losing his sense of self. Everybody's desire is for the other's desire, but with the Hysteric, says Lacan, this desire is always *unfulfilled*. The Hysteric's temptation implies no commitment to fulfillment. His position as subject is threatened by the other's jouissance and he has no intention of fulfilling it.

Another paradox derives from the Hysteric's way of dealing with his own desire. Positioning as *objet a*, the Hysteric instates the other as superior and turns to him with the enigma of his own desire. This undermines both his authority as agent of knowledge and his sense of reality: the Other has no answers. She too is lacking. We can see here the large *epistemic* dimension in the drama of the Hysteric's life. He is studiously and meticulously exploring the question of desire. This is how Lacan puts it in Seminar 5: "What is the desire of my hysteric? ... Any hysteric echoes everything related to the question about desire as it appears in others, even in a latent manner ... of posing the question" (Lacan 1957–1958, pp.466–7). Hysteria is not only a structure, but also a role, calling for a perpetual reaching beyond (Gherovici 2009, Fink 1995). This perpetual questioning undermines the stability of the big Other and its pressure for conformity.

One can also understand the Hysteric's way of representing lack through the metaphor of sexual difference. If lack defines a subject, it follows that the lack of the penis in sexual difference defines the woman in the Imaginary, thus tying up the feminine with lack. The Hysteric, anatomically male or female, is frustrated by the Symbolic lack he sustains by not being the mother's phallus. His identity is always in question form: 'What is a woman?' or 'Am I a man or a woman?' (Lacan 1955–1956). Feeling unjustly deprived of the phallus, he can delegate the question of this lack only to someone who is supposed to have it. This 'someone' is, in fact, the name-of-the-father, the ultimate master. In that sense, the Hysteric accepts the law, yet repeatedly contests it because he will not receive answers to the enigmas of origin, of desire and of sexual difference.

5.4 Perversion

The Obsessive and the Hysteric, as neurotics, have undergone castration and desire is the epicenter of their quest for identity. Their various maneuvers represent attempts to eradicate effects of separation and lack. In contradistinction, Lacan's Pervert is only partly castrated. He is situated firmly in language but has never fully separated from the mother. Thus, he is in a position of *denying* lack rather than *repressing* the knowledge of it. Accordingly, his quest revolves around jouissance.

While the Obsessive denies lack by pretending he owns *objet a*, and the Hysteric plays a circular game of 'plugging' and revealing the lack in the Other, the Pervert *cancels* lack by regressing to, or maintaining, the position of the Other's phallus. The Pervert's relations are shaped by *being an object* for the other. The Hysteric and the Pervert both occupy the role of *objet a* in relation to the Other, but there is an important difference between them: the Hysteric positions himself as the **object-cause** of the Other's desire and evades jouissance, while the Pervert poses as the **satisfying object** of the Other's desire, namely, as the Other's object of jouissance. The partner of both is a lacking Other, but the Hysteric sustains the Other's lack, whereas the Pervert cancels it.

The Pervert moves between making himself or the other the object of jouissance. He does not care whether he locates as subject or object of intercourse, because he has not acquired any preference in this respect. For example, "The sadist himself occupies the place of the object ... to the benefit of another, for whose *jouissance* he exercises his action as sadistic pervert" (Lacan 1963–1964, p.185). Unlike the neurotic, he is not plagued by questions and *knows* both sides of desire. The other is essentially a puppet in a fixed ceremonial script that provides perverse satisfaction. If the other is incapable of playing his part, the Pervert immediately replaces him.

In perversion, the small, specular other is an object of manipulation, a means or instrument. This renders him replaceable or even superfluous, as in some forms of fetishism. When the Pervert acts as object of the other's jouissance, he feels obliged to comply even if it means breaking the law. In that sense, *the other precedes the Other*. Jouissance precedes the law. In Lacan's words, "The Lord's will be done" (Ibid, p.229). The beauty of this formulation is that it holds for subject and other both at the same time. Thus, the Pervert can identify either with the pre-Oedipal mother or with his object (always a small, narcissistic part-object), repeating the scene of early infancy when, as Lacan sees it, all mothers perversely treat their child in ways that suit their jouissance. It is up to the paternal function to limit the mother's jouissance and liberate the child. Alas, the paternal function is not internalized in the Pervert's structure, so no proper Other exists in his world. The Pervert's world is mastered by a *primal* father-mother, *experienced* as Other. Yet, this Other remains other as he himself is not subjected to the law.

Perversion, like other clinical structures, may be generalized and analyzed in the terms of social roles. As such, the Pervert inclines to totalitarianism and may inflict much suffering through violent and cruel implementation of his ruler's imperatives. Hannah Arendt (1963) describes how horrible it had been for the Nazis to execute Jews personally, but they found comfort knowing that they were doing their duty to lord and country. The Pervert situates himself as the pure instrument of the other: He carries no responsibility, he is an instrument, fulfilling the Other's Will. Guilt and doubt are the painful privileges of neurosis. Since neurotic structure generally implies a question, it inherently offers the *possibility* of innovation. The Pervert does not require investigation or imagination to validate his knowledge. Unlike the revolutionary neurotic, he acts like the meticulous administrator.[2]

Žižek sees perversion as residing

> ... in the formal structure of how the subject relates to truth and speech. The Pervert claims direct access to some figure of the big Other (from God and history to the desire of his partner) so that, dispelling all the ambiguity of language, he is able to act directly as the instrument of the big Other's will.
>
> (Žižek 2016)

This is why Žižek saw Osama bin Laden and President Bush as sharing a Perverted structure: They both believed their acts were directly ordained by divine will.

Žižek relates perversion to a unique differentiation between desire and drive. Desire contains its own regulative ideal. The subject is required to renounce the Thing and accept alternative satisfactions. This is how the pleasure principle works, balancing anxiety and jouissance by maintaining a proper distance from *objet a*. The subject of the drive, in contradistinction, denies the partiality of stand-ins, treating them as transcendental fillers of the void (Žižek 2008). This traps him in a repetitive circuit of jouis-sance that does not answer to the pleasure principle and creates a self-propelling, endless loop. Žižek shows with great clarity how the perverse dynamic feeds capitalism. While the Hysteric finds that the capitalist marketplace coheres with the incomplete nature of his desire, the Pervert taps into capitalism on a more funda-mental level. The whole capitalist machinery is propelled by an impersonal compulsion to engage in the circular movement of (re)production. This happens when the circulation of money as capital becomes 'an end in itself' (Žižek 2016), acting according to its own total knowledge. This social perversion dispossesses us as subjects.

The Pervert's relation to the other indicates where the other *splits* into pre- and post-Oedipal manifestations. Lacan notes that the Pervert's relation with his pre-Oedipal, omnipotent mother revels in jouissance while, simultaneously, engaging the post-Oedipal Other to limit it. This is enacted when the Pervert offers himself as object of jouissance, while also asserting meticulous 'laws' that limit it. Contrary to this ceremonious pseudo-lawfulness, but still pronouncing the law, the Pervert exceeds his partner's limits by acting out in public. This enacts the perverted tension between the pre- and post-Oedipal others.

5.5 Psychosis

The Psychotic is someone who forecloses the name-of-the-father, removing it from an active role in her psychic economy. This means that she has not undergone castration and has not sepa-rated from her pre-Oedipal (m)other. Neither did she undergo alienation in language. Having rejected the Symbolic element, she dwells permanently in the dimensions of the Imaginary and the Real. She experiences intense inner rupture and permeability; anyone can penetrate her, confuse or confiscate her internal organs. Others can see what she is thinking or feeling and implant thoughts in her mind.

The Psychotic's perpetual sense of danger is augmented by lack of differentiation and may be described through a quote from Seminar 17:

> ... the desire of the mother ... is not something one can stand
> like that, indifferently. It always causes disaster. A big croco-
> dile in whose mouth you are ... One never knows whether she
> will suddenly decide to snap her trap shut. ... It is the [phallic]
> roller which protects you should the jaws suddenly close.
>
> (Lacan 1969–1970, p.129)

The Psychotic, at any moment, may be devoured and obliterated.
Being the object of jouissance in ways she cannot control, she is
usually cast in a passive position, reminiscent of Schreber's position
in relation to God's passion (Freud 1911).

In the mirror stage, the subject gains a body image. Passing
from the Imaginary to the Symbolic, the body is rewritten by
Symbolic signifiers; it gets differentiated and appears in language,
when body parts receive their normative names and functions.
This also involves the evacuation of jouissance from the body as a
whole into limited, particular erotogenic zones. Lacking both
agency and Symbolic structuring, the Psychotic cannot control his
sensations and experiences himself perpetually flooded by painful,
ecstatic jouissance.

The absence of the paternal metaphor is tied up with a failure
of primal repression and unconscious functioning. Consequently,
the Psychotic experiences intimidating, disavowed thoughts that
appear from the outside in the form of hallucinations. Trapped in
the Imaginary, the Psychotic is given to impulsive waves of infatuation and aggressivity, with no ability to resort to the law for
defense or to triadic space for refuge. Her confusion between
herself and the feared (and desired) other drives her to destroy
the other (and herself), as characteristic of the Imaginary. Lacan
has provided the remarkable case study of Aimee (Lacan 1967,
pp.137–9), a paranoid Psychotic who felt that people derived
pleasure in hurting her baby. Experiencing her baby and herself
as objects of the other's jouissance, and in the absence of Symbolic law, Aimee resorted to Real acts of violence intended to
limit the hurtful people's jouissance.

All signifiers are anchored and ordered by the master signifier,
the name-of-the-father. When it is foreclosed, the signifiers no
longer function as linguistic elements that form coherent meanings

according to syntactic rules. The Psychotic does not experience himself as *speaking*, but rather as *spoken* by language. This manifests neatly in hebephrenic schizophrenia, where the 'hole' in the Symbolic is reproduced as holes in the subject, creating fragmented and incoherent signifying chains, complemented by unruly signifiers that act as *things*. Coherent signification and communication are thus undermined, as is the identity of both self and other. The absent paternal metaphor dictates the complete absence of metaphoric structure in the Psychotic's psyche, to the extent that even her symptoms lack Symbolic significance. In a universe of dyadic logic and symbolic equations, the Psychotic experiences only arbitrary certainties. Everything relates to her personally. Neutral happenings, like rainfall, acquire malicious, self-centered signification.

Verhaeghe (2004) argues that Lacanian logic advocates the treatment of Psychotics by producing *anchoring points* that realize the ordering function of the lacking master signifier. This could consist of establishing a firm identification with the analyst, alongside well-defined practices and adherence to clear rules. The primary aim of treatment becomes the restoration of the primary relation between the subject and the Other as law. In Verhaeghe's terms, Psychotics don't need 'subject analysis', but rather 'subject amplification', in the form of stable structures (Ibid, p.309).

In this manner, we can establish clear Lacanian practices for the differential treatment of the various clinical structures. For example, with the Hysteric, who tries to tune into and accommodate the Other's desire, the analyst should frustrate her effort to know the Other's desire (e.g., through visual or auditory information). Likewise, because the Obsessive tends to nullify the Other, the analyst might mark her presence by conspicuous body movement or loud breathing. This may nudge the patient towards perceiving the existence of the Other and his desire. When, as clinicians, we begin to see patients as structured by lack, desire and jouissance, rather than as a collections of symptoms, we may grapple with the structural components here and now, freeing desires trapped in circuits of suffering. This may loosen ego identifications and transform them in the hope of allowing the patient to enjoy more freely.

Notes

1 We designate the Lacanian use of the term by capitalizing it.
2 See also: *The Conformity of Perversion*, Kirsten Hyldgaard, https://www.lacan.com/conformper.htm

Chapter 6

Sexuation

6.1 Sexuality according to Freud

Freud and Lacan were heavily criticized for the seeming phallocentrism of their construal of sexual difference. Freudian sexual development hinges on castration anxiety following the discovery of the sexual difference between girls and boys. It is at this moment that the penis, the anatomical limb, acquires its value

> as a symbol this time, in so far as its absence or presence transforms an anatomical distinction into a major yardstick for the categorization of human beings, and in so far as, for each individual subject, this absence or presence is not taken for granted and remains irreducible to a mere *datum* ...
>
> (Laplanche & Pontalis 1988)

The Freudian penis became a general marker of difference. Importantly, Freud never proposed that this difference offers a clear definition of either masculine or feminine sexuality.

He writes: "... psycho-analysis cannot elucidate the intrinsic nature of what in conventional or in biological phraseology is termed 'masculine' and 'feminine': it simply takes over the two concepts and makes them the foundation of its work" (Freud 1920, p.171). Sexuality is foundational for psychoanalysis because, for Freud, it is a general force of life, an innate drive and an element of the unconscious. But the unconscious does not represent sexual difference, so Freud was only able to say that unconscious

DOI: 10.4324/9781003106883-6

sexuality amounts to innate bisexuality. Note that 'bisexuality' appears 44 times in Freud's work (Perelberg 2005), but a firm definition of its forming elements is not given anywhere. For Freud, assuming a sexual identity involves a long, intricate intra- and inter-subjective process.

As Freud describes in startlingly postmodern terms, the concept of 'sexuality' covers a wide spectrum of features concerning sexual behavior and develops from the interaction among three independent dimensions: anatomy (penis, vagina, physical hermaphroditism), mental sexual characteristics (roughly equivalent to gender) and object choice. The sources and development of these dimensions do not overlap. While anatomy is given, mental qualities develop during childhood through identifications, especially those of the Oedipal stage. Due to our innate bisexuality, the Oedipal complex has both positive and negative versions. The former involves creating an erotic attachment to the opposite-sexed parent, while perceiving the same-sexed parent as rival. The latter involves the erotic attachment to the same-sexed parent with the opposite-sexed parent perceived as rival. The *mental* aspect of sexuality will be determined by the interaction between the relative strength of the innate sexual elements and differential identifications with each parent. This process also influences object choice. As can be seen already in Freud's formulations, the accepted binary structure of sexuality is subverted and the triangular space of sexuality may create variations of trans- and homosexuality, in addition to normative heterosexuality. For example, Freud writes with remarkable clarity about a feminine mind in a male body who desires anatomical men of female gender (Freud 1920).

In the development of sexual identity, elements contrary to the chosen sex are repressed, but they can resurface at later points in life. In that sense, the shaping of sexuality is life-long and may re-emerge in different forms. All-in-all, sexuality is inherently heterogeneous and includes gaps, breaks and interruptions. It is upon this basis that Lacan begins his work on sexuation. Freud had already subverted the traditional debate between culture and nature in the genesis of sexual identity. Lacan picked up where Freud had left off: he undertook to characterize gender[1] in terms of desire and jouissance.

6.2 Reconceptualizing the phallus and castration

While Freudian castration hinges on the penis as limb and manifests differently in boys and girls, Lacanian castration is anatomy-
free and involves a separation from the mother and alienation in
language. For Lacan, the father is the cornerstone of the Symbolic
and the mother's Imaginary object of desire. But why did he chose
the phallus to designate this situation? Let us examine this from
the vantage point of sexual development.

From the moment the phallus appears in the child's psychic life,
it serves as *signifier* rather than a limb. The Oedipal child,
according to Lacan, under the influence of maternal symbiosis, is
immersed in the maternal Thing, but does not possess a clear
sense of otherness. Otherwise, he would not need to 'be' this
something (the phallus) to act as the mother's exclusive object.
There is an absent, unknown otherness here whose only relevance
is the mother's desire. Lacan marks it by the Greek letter φ (phi):
the primitive signifier of the phallus. φ, like any other representation, indicates absence of an object that is replaced by the presence of a sign. This ultimate and exclusive object of desire does
not exist anywhere except in the child's fantasy and has nothing to
do with male or any other anatomy.

Why then call it 'the phallus'? We suggest that there are a few
reasons for this. Firstly, Lacan wanted to retain affinities with
Freud, even when he undermined the original meanings. The use
of the word 'phallus' is a prime example here. Secondly, Lacan
makes a sophisticated, subversive choice of a concept that, on one
hand, acts as a cornerstone for sexual difference but, on the other
hand, is entirely unreal. The phallus is a monarch whose reign is
achieved through abdication. This comes through even in replacing the word 'phallus' with the letter φ. It is a figment of the
child's Imaginary, an order of illusion and deceit that creates
structure and integrity where they do not exist, causing fraudulent
misrecognitions of non-existent perfection. It is in that realm of
pseudo-perfection that Lacan places the phallus, thereby inherently undermining its validity. It is only in the Imaginary that the
fleeting, temporary erect mode of an ordinarily limp and fleshy
organ can be granted the illusory strength of eternity. The erect

form of the penis is secondary from the perspective of probabilities; it is erect for only a fraction of its tenure as a living entity. *The tenure of the phallus is always under duress.* For Lacan, this is the formative element of castration anxiety. Rather than being a threat of de-capitation, **it is the reality of a destined lack**.

The Lacanian "phallus is the privileged signifier of this mark in which the role of logos is wedded to the advent of desire" (Lacan 1967, p.581). The φ, in its more developed form as name-of-the-father, draws its strength not from the realm of anatomy, but from the realm of the signifier. It indicates the possibility of signifying absence and potentially granting meaning to desire. The phallus is unique in not signifying anything but possibilities of signification. It is unrelated to any fixed meaning. As signifier of signification, it serves as meta\master-signifier (what Freud (1915) termed 'vorstellungrepresentanz'. See also Herera 2010). By holding no specific meaning (only the potential for it), the phallus acts as an empty vessel, a vase whose essence is to be empty. Only this lack, this absence of fullness, creates a master *signifier* out of a shape that could otherwise be a mere object (Lacan 1967, pp.575–84).

It is in relation to *this* phallus as signifier that sexual difference – Lacan's term is 'sexuation' – is determined. That sexuation occurs only with the advent into the Symbolic is logically self-evident, because only in the Symbolic difference exists. Lacan's differentiation of the masculine and feminine is determined by the way the subject positions herself in relation to the master signifier and the phallic function it represents, i.e. Symbolic law. The phallic *function* regulates desire and jouissance, and the asymmetry between men and women receives its final signature and expression as differences in forms of desire and jouissance.

6.3 Sexuation

Sexuation is inherent in the transition from ideal ego to desiring subject (Lacan 1972–1973). And yet, it may change throughout a subject's life as it involves the subject's active positioning (see Hadar 2022). Lacanian gender is, at least potentially, a *process* rather than an assertion.

In Seminar 20 Lacan presents his comprehensive account of sexuation. Roughly formulated, masculinity is characterized by the complete subjection of desire and jouissance to phallic-Symbolic law, whereas femininity can transcend it. These differences are given in logical formulas which we now present and explain. The formulae that appear in the sexuation diagram (Figure 6.1) are based on two logical functions – the existential (∃) and the universal (∀) quantifiers – together with the phallic function (Φ). They convey their message in a mixture of analysis and metaphor. Let us examine how the diagram works.

a. The upper boxes

The upper boxes provide the definition of 'Man' and 'Woman', with man on the left and woman on the right. We shall refer to their Lacanian definition with initial capital letters: Man and Woman.

Man: The 'Man' box says (upper line) 'There exists an X for which the phallic function doesn't apply', and on the lower line it says 'For every X the phallic function applies'. Why does Lacan define sexuation in a way that seems contradictory?

Lacan clearly suggests that the logic that applies for sexuation is of a different nature than school logic. Here, the validity of the universal quantifier depends on an exception. 'Translated' into psychoanalytic language, the formulae convey that, in the male category, there must exist a subject not given to the jurisdiction of Symbolic law (i.e. the phallic function, marked here by Φ). This would be a Psychotic, or a person resembling the primal father – someone free of the law's limitations, including the law forbidding

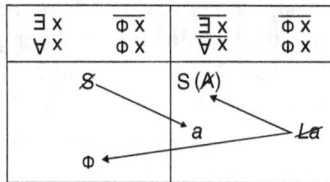

Figure 6.1 Sexuation

incest. This means being unlimited in desire (who and how much we want) and jouissance (how we want it). All other subjects in the category of Man are *wholly* given to the Symbolic law. In Freudian language this implies that they have resolved the Oedipal complex, and constructed and abstracted their superego. Anatomically determined women may belong in the male category if they are either: 1. Psychotic or omnipotent and free of the law's limits, as the pre-Oedipal mother is sometimes portrayed, or: 2. Subjects whose desire and jouissance are determined by the imperatives of the Oedipal law.

In accordance with the signifier's logic, Man holds the positions of knowledge, language and authority. His modes of jouissance are wholly determined by the law. Within this frame, hierarchies may be defined and a perfect (non-lacking) Subject may be Imagined. This leads Ragland-Sullivan (1992) to speak about an 'Imaginary Symbolic', an idealized object of identification who has a linguistic representation, an Imaginary figure and a fantasized personality. When Man enters the Symbolic, his Imaginary body undergoes a makeup according to the normative conventions of sexuality and gender. The polymorphous jouissance of old is held at bay and restructured by the effects of language and arbitrary, gendered fictions. Since culture sees sexual difference as arising from anatomical difference, the phallus and the penis may collapse and their differences obliterated in the 'Imaginarized' Symbolic realm of the Man. He then experiences himself as a knowing, comprehensive whole. Stated differently, Lacan is actually taking the Symbolic to task for preserving mythic versions of idealized forms. This is what leads anatomical males to experience themselves as whole, pure men, repressing that part of themselves from which they had detached and which had left them lacking: the feminine, maternal body.

Woman: The 'Woman' upper line says that 'There does not exist an X for which the phallic function does not apply', while the lower line says that 'Not for every X does the phallic function apply'.

The second formula of Woman is semantically equivalent to the first formula of Man. Yet, its temporal positioning in regard to its counterpart determines its difference from Man's first formula. Like Man, in order to be sexuated, Woman has to be a Symbolic subject under the phallic law (marked by the Φ function), i.e., a subject who has accepted the law set down by the name-of-the-father. Again, the second formula contradicts the first, stating that there are subjects to which the phallic function *does not* apply. Transferring the matheme into Lacanian narrative may circumvent contradiction by temporally positioning the second formula as signifying an event *coming after* the first formula. This may mean that, after achieving the status of Symbolic subject, women take an *additional* step, where the Symbolic is subverted. Thus, a Woman does not define herself only in terms of what Symbolic law dictates or allows. A Woman exceeds the Symbolic; she may live her desire and jouissance in ways that do not align with the phallic function, thus becoming a subject-with-a-remainder, an excessive subject, a re-opened set.

The idea that Woman may exceed language and law marks her trajectory towards the Real. This accords with Lacan's growing insight about how subjecthood (and therapy) may gain by 'intentionally' incorporating the Real (Miller 1997). It is here that Lacan returns to the differentiation of thought and being. In order to become a speaking, thinking subject, being had to be sacrificed ('the money or your life' sort of thing). In the category of Woman, the subject gets another shot at being, as we now describe.

b. The lower boxes

In the lower box of Man we meet two familiar signifiers: the split/barred subject *ß* and the phallic function Φ. In the lower box of Woman we find two additional signifiers: The *objet a* of the fundamental fantasy and the signifier of the barred Other, S(Å). Who is this barred Other? After the name-of-the-father separated from the merged mother-child dyad, each of the dyad's constituents splits into two. The barred Other is the equivalent of the barred subject. Thus *ß* and Å mark, respectively, the child and the (m) Other, both lacking, after castration. This lacking Other differs from the big Other of old: it stands for the pre-Oedipal, omnipotent mother (the one the Pervert is still attached to as an object of jouissance) or as the name-of-the-father, that ego Ideal who, in the eyes of the child, had what the Ideal ego did not. This is the big Other the obsessive obeys while refusing its authority; the Hysteric is adamant to instate this big Other only in order to then bring him down. This big Other has something that makes him superior and the subject must answer to his demand. In his capacity as name-of-the-father, he acts as superego (Lacan 1957–1958), ordering the world as we know it. Relations with him are often conflictual, manifesting in experiences of subjugation, rebellion, transgression and guilt. He is perpetually perceived as telling the subject what, when and how to do things. The subject tends to experience his word as imperative. **He** might be Rabbi or pastor, father, professor or boss. **He** might also be a righteous peer, perpetually making one feel ashamed and worthless. **He** might be the doctor, cruelly dictating treatments. **He** might even be the watch that forces me to wake in the morning and reprimands me for the time I have wasted, making me want to hide from its face. This big Other is everywhere. He installs compulsions into my life, a feeling that I *must* do this thing or the other. On the heels of the 'must', guilt appears, because often I *don't* do what I must. This familiar neurotic relation is a monarch-subject relation. One can obey or disobey, but one knows her place. This is the Other who has made one a subject.

The question to be asked, as in any economy, is: What does one get out from this deal? Why does one agree to subject oneself in such a manner? To feeling guilty and unworthy? The Sartrean answer to this concerns our complex relations with freedom. We are used to upholding freedom as a precious ideal, downplaying the existential fact that it is also extremely anxiety provoking. Freedom entails making choices and taking responsibility. It demands a self-discipline that one is free of when told what to do. Having a big Other gives one her identity that is predicated upon the alienation of desire and submission of authenticity, yet it gives the subject the frame of security and direction. For Freud, these are the needs that motivated man's invention of God. As long as **He** exists, I have someone who guides me and takes responsibility. I have someone who 'owes' me, someone whom I can approach as deserving of something.

With a lacking Other I cannot do all this. He is no longer omnipotent or omniscient, and I am no longer entitled, blaming or blamed, guilty or guided. I am on a par with him or her. Losing my big Other, I may be orphaned, but I have gained my freedom and potential possibilities with my barred and lacking Others: equality, friendship, comradery, and perhaps even – we will get there soon – love. This barred Other has always existed. He is like myself, but it took me time to become aware of him and acknowledge his existence. In the diagram of sexuation we encounter him as desired by Woman.

Beyond the phallus, the void of the other is no longer concealed by a permanent, arbitrary signifier that masquerades as presence. It is an absence that we must, and may, signify but, inasmuch as we are Woman, we can shape these significations in an individual way, allow our desired other his own signification. Being Woman does not require one to submit oneself to universal significations. She offers an alternative to phallic discourse in being particular, even singular, in her use of language.

Lacan marked this singularity by writing the French definite article, 'La' (at the heart of the box) in crossed-out form: La. He expressed this idea in various forms, one of which is especially provocative: *The woman does not exist* (Lacan 1972–1973). To wit, this does not imply that there is no such thing as woman; it implies that woman is not a universal or uniform category; that every woman will find a particular, significant way in which she will signify *desire* (the element of absence in self and Other) and practice it. **The** woman does not exist because it is impossible to predict, or even know, how she will subvert the Symbolic. Whereas one may describe **the** Man and thus refer to all subjects in this category, in the category of woman one may describe **a** woman, and then another woman and another, but this category does not have a prototype. It is comprised of individuals. We believe that this is an early articulation of queer theory, namely, of the idea that gender is not binary. Woman's category consists of endless potential disseminations that diverge from any (phallic) norm.

Another way of understanding the signifier of the barred other (S(Å)) involves its procedural character. It heralds the 'know-how' we discuss in the next chapter. 'Know-how' is a kind of knowledge that cannot be verbally articulated, but rather acted or performed. It bears a resemblance to 'procedural memory' in cognitive psychology, namely, the kind of knowledge that allows us to ride a bike or swim. It also may sub-serve the kind of *performativity* that Butler suggests as giving rise to gender (Butler 1990). Briefly, Butler thought that gender is a matter of choice, a manner of doing things rather than an intrinsic category of social positioning. In her logic, gender is determined by behavior: characteristic modes of speech, typical gait or limb movement, modes of dressing, etc. In contemporary culture, Butler claims, we must be either one gender or the other in order to be considered as subjects. Hence, it is possible that a 'Butlerian' woman who is aware of the arbitrary, contingent nature of the Symbolic, its laws and categories, will perform its prescribed behaviors differently, or even defiantly, in order to subvert the Symbolic categorization of her gender. Such performance does not demand explanation, formulation, or even thought. It is, rather, already an expression of knowledge and a construction of alternative knowledge. Butler becomes somewhat of a Lacanian when, in her innovative inflection of verbs, she neatly illustrates how knowledge-in-action may subvert normative, ossified categories of knowledge. She says, "I have been being a lesbian for twenty years now" (Butler 1993). The syntax here conveys the performativity of being lesbian.

6.4 There is no sexual relation

For Lacan, sexuality is situated in the gaps of absence and instability, in the dialectics of desire, ever reaching, never arriving. Now, in psychoanalysis meaning is sexual, but this can be true only when the limits of meaning are taken into account. Meaning, like the subject herself "... indicates the direction in which it fails" (Lacan 1967, p.416). It exists only at its moment of failure. *That* is where sexuality begins yet, contrary to its subversive nature, sexuality tends to be discussed in Imaginary terms, namely, as a relationship.

Freud construed sexuality as both polymorphous and traumatic, yet he believed in a phylogenetic, universal psychosexual scheme of development that culminates in the potential ability to create mature and lasting relation in the realm of genitality. The idea that sexual relations establish a singular kind of complementary whole is common in Western culture and has also been promoted by the three monotheistic religions (e.g. Prudence 2020)[2]. Lacan saw this as a sad joke: It is not only wrong; it is a ploy society uses in order to discipline its subjects. For Lacan, it is fraudulent to assume that desire is divided in a categorical manner (along gendered lines) and that, moreover, it is both complementary and mutual. Such a view represents a regression to the Imaginary illusions of wholeness and totality, denying the basic truth of the irredeemable division of the Symbolic subject. Anatomy and reproduction may point to gender complementarity, but they have nothing to do with the essence of Lacanian sexuation: Man is not necessarily the object of Woman's desire and vice versa. Lacan gave this idea a succinct and provocative expression: *There is no (such thing as a) sexual relationship.* Of course there are relations between people which involve sex. But it is not upon them that a 'sexual relation' hinges. What 'sexual relation' implies is the existential fit between the desires of sexuated humans, while Lacan thought that *the desires of Man and Woman run parallel to each other.* In Figure 6.1, this is indicated by the arrows that cross the lines of the lower boxes. Here, Man's desire is indicated by the arrow leading from $\bar{s}$ (on Man's side) toward the *objet a* (on Woman's side).

Notice that this connection echoes the basic fantasy, drawing an equivalence between Man's desire and the general pattern of desiring in the Symbolic. We will outline this pattern here as it relates to the sexual relation, or rather as it relates to its impossibility. Man, in his search for *objet a*, seeks what will make him whole, what will undo his lack. This is what ordinarily causes Symbolic subjects to confuse the cause of their desire with its object, thus inevitably meeting disappointment. In the realm of sexual relations and in line with the neurotic plight, the 'it' found in love is rarely "It!", beyond the moment of conquest. In the following moment, 'It' is inevitably unveiled in its Imaginary guise.

An additional feature of Imaginary desiring is its narcissistic character. The subject desires *his own perfection.* The other is measured in terms of his ability to deliver a precious object he seems to possess that I badly need. This mode of desiring is effectually an objectification of the other, which does not allow truly entertaining one's subjectivity. It is also a reduction of the desire to need, which further ensures the impossibility of satisfaction.

Disappointments are further magnified by the manner in which culture reinforces the Imaginary illusion of complementarity. In endless myths, fairytales, movies and love songs, loving is described as the immersion of self in the other. Yet, this drive towards oneness – wanting to be one with the other, feeling that one *has* someone under her skin – entails the death of a subject, either of one's own self or of the other. For example, consider the sentence 'You take my breath away'. It tries to capture the experience of recognizing the person that one is in love with. Another example concerns the well-known term for orgasm in French, 'la petit morte' – the small death (of the subject). Further, we create 'Cinderella syndromes' by reading fairytales about royal salvation of the lady in distress. In this case, both the lady and the prince serve as *objet a* for each other. Or the little boy who watches Disney movies ending with the prince's transformation from frog to prince. He might be bitterly disappointed in the future to discover that real kisses do not engender such transformations. Cultural conditioning causes us to live out some dangerous, harmful fiction, necessarily objectifying the other as one forces their needs upon him. Looking to the other in order to fix one's inherent, constitutive lack reinforces one's disappointment.

Lacan calls Man's jouissance 'phallic' because it is linked to a part of the body (also called 'jouissance of the limb or organ'). This indicates both its quantitative limitation and the false emphasis on the genitals as providing complementarity. Woman also entertains phallic jouissance, but she has something extra, a 'remainder'. This lifts the limitations (both quantitative and genital) and allows her to experience 'surplus jouissance', namely, a jouissance that incorporates the Symbolic and Real elements, which both create and dissolve significations (see below).

6.5 Feminine desire and jouissance

While Man desires *objet a*, Woman desires two things, as indicated by the two crossing arrows in the diagram: The phallic function and the barred Other. The former is a fairly simple desire to have her place in the world, in the Symbolic order. This marks a desire to exercise her phallic jouissance within recognized frames like sex, speech, marriage, family, or other organized settings. She also craves Symbolic recognition of her gender identity, being addressed as 'miss' or 'Mrs', having rights specific to women (e.g., the right of abortion), etc. The big Other grants her position in the Symbolic, alongside some certainties regarding herself and the world. Woman benefits from her position in relation to the Phallus, yet she is not subjugated to it. This grants her desire the freedom to reach beyond phallic jouissance and extend its limits. Lacan called this 'surplus jouissance'.

In Figure 6.1, the second arrow of desire is directed toward the signifier of the barred Other (S(Ⱥ)). Woman as a subject realizes that the guarantor himself lacks a guarantee: there is no metaphysical backing for the law and the Other representing it, be it Rabbi, God or Nature. A Woman acknowledges lack, both in herself and in her Other. She has, in that sense 'traversed' the fundamental fantasy in a way we will discuss in the next chapter. She assumes her *objet a* as lack, and has renounced the fantasy of being complete. In a world of lacking subjects, she now faces the difficult choices regarding her gender positioning. She may now seek another Woman who has likewise embraced her lack and who may arouse her and offer her own desire in return. Neither of the two need to have female genitalia in order to sexuate as a Woman. They only need to position in relation to the phallic function (Symbolic law) that determines sexuation. The Man is any subject who is totally given to the law and can derive *only* phallic (organ related) jouissance. A Woman has modes of jouissance that are independent of the organ and not necessarily aligned with Symbolic conventions.

Woman enjoys "a jouissance of the body that is, if I may express myself thus – ... beyond the phallus" (Lacan 1972–1973, p.148), that is, exceeding the Symbolic, its laws and meanings. This "... jouissance that is hers (à elle), that belongs to that 'she' (elle) who doesn't exist and doesn't signify anything. She perhaps knows nothing about this jouissance, but she experiences it – that much she knows. She knows it, of course, when it comes (arrive). It doesn't happen (arrive) to all of them" (Ibid, p.74). The 'elle' doesn't signify because she exceeds zones of signification, of knowledge. This is why her jouissance may be experienced, yet not be known. This subversion, this transcending step 'beyond', is possible only after securing her footing in Symbolic jouissance.

It is difficult to formulate in Symbolic terms a jouissance 'of the body' that exceeds the Symbolic. But of course, language is not only Symbolic and has Imaginary and Real dimensions. Lacan formulates the surplus in relation to mysticism and the letter, both of which return us to the body's materiality. This is available to anatomic males, because men are "just as good as women ... Despite – I won't say their phallus – despite what encumbers them that goes by that name". Men who have "... a jouissance that is beyond ... are the ones we call *mystics*" (Ibid, p.151). In Judaism, for example, the rational hermeneutic Rambam refused to describe God in positive terms, as this would assume the ability of man to know him. God may only be described in terms of the negative. This is a way of upholding forever the un-whole knowledge of God as an infinite whole, and also God's own un-wholeness, still using Symbolic means (marked in the negative). This resonates with Lacan's assertion that "Woman cannot be said. Nothing can be said of Woman" (Ibid, p.76), or, "A Woman can but be excluded by the nature of things ..." (Ibid, p.68). The Jewish mystics, the Hasidim, on the other hand, believe that God *may* be known, but this knowledge is not reached by logical thinking. Rather, it may be reached through the kind of ecstatic experiences that only the body may know. We see this in other religions as well, through rites of fasting, chanting, excessive dance and self-flogging.

Lacan discusses *the letter* in relation to feminine jouissance. This letter is not the signifier of law and meaning, but rather the *materiality of the signifier*, namely, its Real dimension. The letter, like Woman, resides outside common knowledge. Both may carry the 'knowledge without a subject', the extra-phallic that inhabits the unconscious, that part "of the unconscious that cannot be spoken" (quoted in Mitchell & Rose (1982, p.53)). Being a Woman does not allow docking to any identification; one does not recognize oneself in it, so much so that it induces the feeling of being Other for oneself. In this indeterminate realm of choices, a Woman finds the angst and joy of freedom, and will inscribe her choices in the loci of the indeterminate signifier: the letter.

The letter allows devious significations, "spaces of poesis" (Barnard 2002, p.17). It resonates the speech that the third wave of feminism aspires to, embracing ambiguity and non-identity while retaining social contracts and commonality with others (as embodied beings). Kristeva (1984) characterizes as feminine the *semiotic*, namely, the affective, bodily dimension of language. The semiotic facilitates the energetic movement of signification and acts through the materiality of language, for example, through tonal and rhythmic qualities.

In this *realm of the letter*, beyond articulated knowledge, Lacan situates Truth. If Freud based his conception of woman on how she is socially constructed, Lacan bases his on Man's deconstruction, his ability to outstrip himself as a speaking being. Lacan refers in this context to Marx's notion of 'surplus value' (Marx 1887), the value that allows economic growth. By analogy, it might be that surplus (feminine) jouissance holds the transformative power that allows *subjective* growth.

6.6 Love

In the context of Lacan's discussion of transference love, we will briefly discuss here some general statements about Lacanian love and simultaneously ease our way into the subject of therapy. In Seminar 8, discussing Plato's *Symposium*, Lacan reiterates the myth of Eros's origins. Eros was conceived when Penia, a poor woman, slept beside the rich and drunk Poros on the festive night that celebrated Aphrodite's birth. This myth resonates with the biblical story of Naomi who, after the death of her sons, returns to her homeland with her faithful foreign daughter-in-law Ruth. Naomi tries to dissuade Ruth, telling her that she cannot offer prospects of marriage or a living. Ruth refuses to leave the old woman, declaring that she will share in her destiny, country and faith. Arriving penniless and hungry, the two women follow reapers to gather what remains un-reaped. Spotting them, the rich landowner Boaz instructs his workers to leave plenty for them to gather. The following night Naomi instructs Ruth to lay by Boaz where he sleeps at night by his field hands. This love story ends with the birth of their grandson, King David. David, besides uniting the kingdom so that his son may build the first temple, is described as having beautiful eyes, remarkable musical talent and the ability to capture the hearts of men and women alike. A Jewish Eros of sorts. What is reiterated in these stories is that Eros is not born only of plenty. Love is born of the mixture of poverty and wealth, and there is also a strong contingent element featuring in its origins.

In Seminar 22 Lacan says: "For the one encumbered with a phallus, what is a woman? It is a symptom" (Lacan 1974–1975, p.10). This not only states the ordinary positioning of Woman as *objet a*. Resonating with the repressed desires of Freud's Hysterics, 'symptom' here acts as unclaimed desire that the subject could not incorporate into her Symbolic existence. Woman as symptom redeems Man's desire from being completely covered by the Symbolic, namely, redeems Man from being a semblant of the Symbolic. Even if man is only 'the Man', having a Woman transforms him from being Symbolically closed to being open to non-Symbolic possibilities. This allows him access to other varieties of jouissance and knowledge. The symptom, the traditional flaw, can elevate Man to a realm of love that exceeds the terms of his fundamental fantasy. In the mythologies, it was the flawed Ruth and Penia who, through love, inscribed Boaz and Poros (respectively) in the eternal chain of signifiers.

Elaborating on the theme of poverty and wealth in love, Lacan writes: "... it is that love as such ... – is to give what one does not have ... One cannot love except by becoming a non-haver ... in effect, to give what one has is a festival, it is not love" (Lacan 1960–1961, p.337). He emphasizes that love does not involve the *objet a*: "Between these two terms ... the lover and the beloved, you should notice that there is no coinciding. What is lacking to the one is not this 'what he has', hidden in the other. And this is the whole problem of love" (Ibid, p.33). Lacan is telling us here that there is always a dimension of surprise or contingency in love. You look for something, but you are mistaken in the very thing you are looking for. Ordinarily, you search for *objet a*, which will prove a disappointment by necessity. This thing that you are lacking is *not* what the other has, though it may seem so for a moment.

The reason you stay with someone beyond the moment of disappointment is where things become interesting: "Imagine you see in front of you a beautiful flower, or a ripe fruit. You reach out your hand to grab it. But at the moment you do, the flower, or the fruit, bursts into flames" (Ibid, p.179). Here the *objet a*, the flower or the fruit are gone. But then – "In its place you see another hand appear, reaching back towards your own" (Ibid). Only when the semblants of *objet a* are reduced to ashes, can one recognize someone's seeking (and therefore lacking) subjectivity, reaching out to meet your own.

Love can exist between two subjects who have accepted their lack and stopped conceiving of the other as the holder of *objet a* (the false promise of wholeness). In love, subjects are no longer disappointed with each other, because they stopped blaming the other for their own lack. They may now encounter each other's lacking subjectivity, meet as two barred subjects/others. They may interest each other, formulate, signify and create meanings together. Emotionally and experientially, in love, the condition of lack is tied up with the ability to present the Other with your flaws and vulnerabilities. Your lover does not *search* for your flaws, but when she finds them, they are endearing: the mole on your cheek, your slowness in the morning, the way you twitch your nose when upset. Somehow, this is the way we want to be loved, way beyond our good qualities:

> The person who aspires to be loved is not at all satisfied, as is well known, with being loved for his attributes. He demands to be loved as far as the complete subversion of the subject into a particularity can go ... to love is to love a being beyond what he or she appears to be.
>
> (Lacan 1953–1954, p.276)

The above logic of particularity leads us to believe that flaws determine not only the way in which we want to be loved, but also our object choice. Freud (1927, p.152) describes the excitement in one of his patients, created by a certain "shine on the nose".[3] He interpreted this phenomenon in semantic terms, but we pick it up here in order to discuss *love's support in the Real*. When Lacan

(1961–1962) discusses this '*Glanz auf der nase*', it is in relation to identification through a unary trait. The unary trait, the 'einziger Zug', is "that through which every being is said to be a One, ... designat[ing] the function of unity in so far as ... something is distinguished from what surrounds it ..." (Ibid, p.47). The unary trait identifies something in a way that is not quite Symbolic. The signifier, the prime building block of semiosis in Lacanian theory, requires another signifier in order to create a difference. The unary trait functions on its own and is not governed by the grammar of metonymy and metaphor that rules the ceaseless movement of the signifier. Its origins are related to an "identification ... linked to a certain abandoning of the ... beloved object. This beloved object goes from women to rare books" (Ibid, p.48). The pre-Symbolic unary trait draws its intensity from the moment that the jouissance of merger gives way to the joys of identifying as other (the moment the Ideal ego identifies with the Ego Ideal).

Illustrating love rooted in a unary trait, Lacan tells of his dog's love. The dog meets him in an ecstasy of joy, triggered by no one else, and never mistakes him for anyone else. The dog is clearly not a speaking being. The unary trait that entitles Lacan to her love is his smell, a unique physical quality. It need not be placed next to other scents in order for the dog to recognize him. Notably, in this seminar, Lacan also says that love is always connected to the body, not only in the sense of being narcissistic, but also in bearing a close attachment to the Real.

Returning to our sexuation diagram (Figure 6.1), we can now formulate the conditions for love in the condensed temporality of the Lacanian subject. Notably, the arrows that signify the desire of Men and Women do not intersect, because sexual relations do not exist. Once we understand that sexuation is divorced from anatomy and determined by positioning in relation to the phallic function, we can imagine where intersections may still occur. It will never be in the realms of sense and meaning or the confines of the fundamental fantasy. Neither would it be in the illusions of complementary wholes. Our trajectory may cross that of the other when we accept ourselves and our other as lack, as redundant ashes. Clearly, the nodal point of such intersection is given in the *objet a*, where we offer what we don't have to someone who doesn't want it. We then appear in our vulnerabilities and love the flaws of the other. Such contingencies, anchored in the Real, allow us to move out of narcissistic attachment and impregnate ourselves with otherness. Here our very beginnings (when our Ideal ego identified with the unary trait that served as Ego Ideal) meet our possibilities of beyond, in post-Symbolic feminine jouissance.

Notes

1 Lacan never used 'gender'. We use it here for clarity.
2 Within theological culture, this even has a designated term: 'complementarianism' (https://en.wikipedia.org/wiki/Complementarianism).
3 In German, *Glanz auf der nase* – a signifier which Freud links to the English term 'glance' with which the man was familiar from his English upbringing.

Chapter 7

Therapy

As we have tried to show throughout, the *discontent* of the Lacanian subject is intrinsic to subjecthood. Although every individual is unique in some respects, all subjects undergo the same logical moments of subject positioning and alienation in otherness. Their inauguration into the orders of the Imaginary and the Symbolic involves alienation from bodily experience and bodily needs and subjection to the forms imposed by the Other's desires. The desire for the other's desire was the infant's initial ticket to survival and the determining factor of her identity.

The subject is forever haunted by the question, 'What does the other want?' In Lacanian thought, the answer to that question is also an answer to the existential question, 'Who am I?' What the other wants is critical to who I am. In that sense, identity and alienation go hand in hand. The subject depends on an alienating Other for her most fundamental needs: Identity, survival, security, belonging and love. For this to work out, the Other must be experienced as parental, as having extraordinary qualities. His all-pervasiveness veils both his lack and my own. This is fortified in the Imaginary by the drive for completeness and the fundamental fantasy: There once existed a primordial unity of endless jouissance. We may yet re-appropriate it, make it our own, make ourselves whole. At times it seems that culture in its entirety aims to sustain this illusion.

The above state of affairs leads to chronic dissatisfaction of the subject. His desires feel alienated and the Other, who granted us our identity and whose desire we desire, is always also oppressive.

DOI: 10.4324/9781003106883-7

This has multiple clinical manifestations: Anxiety, ennui, depression, shallow desire and lost creativity. The Other can only hide our lack and emptiness by appearing as ideal, in relation to which we always feel nonplussed. This lack is our only certainty and only upon its discovery and acceptance can our desire come to its own and offer us some sense of purpose.

Analysis gives the subject the chance to own up to (or 'assume') some of the effects of the above state of affairs. In analysis, the subject may discover how alienated he is from his desires, how ignorant he is of what he wants, how much he depends on the other. And he has a chance to align his mind-set with the many misfortunes of being human, a speaking being. In a way, the subject must undertake this opening. It is the money or his life. Only psychoanalytic discourse offers him a chance to re-think his identity in a way that is less dependent on the other. He may then be able to rejoin his body and live a fuller sensual life. This is almost like having both his life and his money. Yet, as always, there will be a price to pay and, in analysis, we have a chance to discover what it is and if we wish to pay it.

7.1 Symptom as alienated desire

In Lacanian therapy, as in the life of the subject, desire is the key, the objective, the point of both entry and termination. The objective is to free the subject to live out his alienated desire. Like in Freud's hysterics, these desires are given, trapped and encoded in symptoms, thus granting them their elevated status. Freud believed these desires could be unearthed and re-encountered in analysis. The subject may then either renounce them or decide that, unlike in the past, he can now accept, or as Lacan would put it – 'assume' – his desire.

For this to happen, the symptom needs to be deciphered and rendered meaningful. In Lacanian analysis, meaning is always given in the terms of a dialogue with an other. The analyst asks the analysand 'What do you want?', often leaving him to discover that he wanted what his other desired. For example, an agoraphobic woman was married to a man who travelled much as part of his business. As therapy developed, the woman increasingly braved leaving her house, but her husband developed fears of flying. The woman's agoraphobia seemed to anticipate her husband's desire to keep her close to him. By complying, she avoided the need to face the terror and meanings of her own desire.

Another brief example is of a man who became an accountant in order to enter and take over his father's business. He was unhappy at work, but persisted with it until depression drove him to therapy. Analysis revealed that the man's choice spared him the need to formulate his own desire and gave him a life that was managed by his father's rules. With therapy, the man became more involved with the company's decision-making and his condition alleviated. This dynamic can also work in negative form. One can feel guilty about not doing well at school because his parents work hard to pay his tuition. He seems to be studying because they want him to, but what is his agenda here? Why is he scared of 'assuming' his ambition? Of course, a likely result would be for the man to fail his exams, despite knowing the material well. His only way not to submit to their desire is by not succeeding. But that, apparently, is still easier than facing the question of what he wants, or rather, what he lacks. The role of the analyst is to guide the subject towards questioning her symptoms and unveil the specific jouissance (of both subject and other) that the symptom seeks to answer or fulfil.

7.2 Transference a: What the analyst must be

For Freud, the transference enacts the analysand's neurosis. Transference transforms repressed desires into the present situation and creates a living reality within the analytic setting. This allows the analyst to access the pathological material, interpret it and work through its damaging effects. For Lacan too, transference is an epiphenomenon of desire, but he offers a different account of its role and the way it plays out in analysis.

For Lacan, what ignites the transference and analysis in general, is the *analyst's* desire. The analyst meets a patient who tells of his symptoms. She gets the ego's account of the symptom, the subject's conscious understanding of his symptom. But whatever that narrative may be, it is not there that the analyst is looking for answers. The analyst knows that the questions of desire (of both self and other) are unconscious. The Lacanian analyst listens, but her attention is not given to the grammatical first-person of the statement (the grammatical subject), but rather to the subject of enunciation, namely, the agent who has produced the statement.[1] The subject of enunciation is always present in the analysand's speech and in crucial points interferes with the statement. This is the familiar heart of any psychoanalytic technique. The analyst is alert to slips of the tongue and blunders that give away what the ego was not interested in presenting. This desire of the analyst activates the transference.

The analysand gradually notices that the analyst is not quite listening to *him*. He is listening to something that lies alongside his speech, that envelopes it or is hidden in it. In terms of Schema L, the analyst is not attending the ego's, but rather the Es's, speech. The analysand notices that the analyst knows *where* the answers to his suffering lie, and this instates him as the *subject-supposed-to-know*. As such the analyst becomes the analysand's subject of desire. Why? Because he *has* it, the knowledge.

In the terms of the fundamental fantasy, in analysis, the analysand's unconscious is positioned as the analyst's *objet a*. Her desire ignites the process of therapy. The analysand, coming with the question of his symptom, attributes knowledge of the answer to his analyst, i.e. he positions *his objet a* in the analyst's person. The subject-supposed-to-know is defined in Lacan's early teaching as, "the one … constituted by the analysand in the figure of … his analyst", who is later Imagined as God the Father (Lacan 1967–1968, p.39). This mutual enactment of the *objet a* (transference) creates love between the analytic pair. Here the analyst must become wary of the dangers awaiting her.

Early on, Freud warned the analyst never to be vain enough to imagine that it is actually herself whom the analysand desires. Transference love reflects libidinal cathexis of parental figures, displaced onto the analyst's person. For Lacan this love is not content-dependent. Rather, it is *structurally* determined through the fundamental fantasy. Lacan warns the analyst – positioned as 'she who has it' – against mistaking this fiction for truth and allowing her ego to identify with the analysand's *objet a*. If the analyst falls into these potholes, analysis will get caught up in the Imaginary (the axis of a–a' in Schema L). The sad outcome of this would be that Es will escape the conversation. This would empty the analytic discourse of its prime added value.

7.3 Transference b: The Imaginary gamut or what the analyst must not be

Until the early 1960s, concerning the subject's freedom, Lacan saw Symbolic discourse as the lesser evil compared to Imaginary discourse. Accordingly, the therapeutic task was seen as enhancing Symbolic awareness and easing the grip of the Imaginary on the subject's thought processes. This figured strongly in Lacan's major writings of the 1950s (Lacan 1967). The analyst's task was to facilitate the analysand's recognition that between the symptom's question and the unconscious answer stand his alienated desires: a whole Imaginary gamut, a series of identifications that aim to answer the other's demand. During therapy, the analysand "ends up by recognizing that this being (himself) has never been more than an imaginary construct and that this construct disappoints all his certainties" (Ibid, p.42). Moreover, "in this labour which he undertakes to reconstruct *for another*, he rediscovers the fundamental alienation that made him construct it *like another*, and which has always been destined to be taken from him by another" (Ibid). In other words, the subject gradually acknowledges that he has molded himself as an other's object and that he is hopelessly enmeshed in endless webs of her demands.

These demands provide him with certainties that he desperately needs, but that sadly and paradoxically foreclose his desire: "Although it always shows through demand ... desire is nevertheless beyond demand. It is also shy of another demand in which the subject ... would like not so much to efface his dependence ... as to fix the very being he proposes there" (Ibid, p.530). The statement that the subject's very being is at stake would make one think he would be eager to secure it. But this is where resistance comes in. Persisting with the repression of castration and denial of lack, the subject courts the very thing that stands between himself and his desire – the Imaginary world of demand. Given half a chance, the analysand will jump on the wagon of demand which, in the Imaginary, is also his *analyst*'s demand. He thus further alienates the desire he unconsciously craves to know and live by. Lacan repeatedly shows how certainty and coherence are ever-present temptations of the Imaginary. One searches for them in the eyes of the other.

To avoid these dynamics, the analyst must demand nothing, as well as avoid complying with any demand. She must skirt the whole domain of demand: "[W]hether it intends to frustrate or to gratify, any response to demand in analysis reduces transference to suggestion" (Ibid). The analyst must give up her conscious experiencing and personality, play dead, suspend her Imaginary being so that the analysand will position himself in the direction of the Symbolic. The analysand demands knowledge but, usually, knowing oneself is an Imaginary fiction that may dangerously replace analysis with the analysand's re-education, "for his own good" (Ibid, p.517). The analyst's art hinges on her ability to accept the positioning of subject-supposed-to-know without falling into the Imaginary fallacy of knowing. Historically, the unary trait marked the subject's first ego Ideal, his first Symbolic alienating identification. This leaves its mark on the analysand's demand, addressed to an idealized analyst who acts, in the transference, as an agent of love and knowledge. If analysts answer from this positioning, they reinforce the subject's submission to the fundamental fantasy and, consequently, reinforce the pattern of idealization and identification. Desire will then remain foreclosed behind the concealment of lack.

In Seminar 8 (Lacan 1960–1961), Lacan uses Alcibiades' infatuation with Socrates to illustrate transference love and explain the position of the analyst's desire. Alcibiades is beautiful and heroic, yet perpetually traitorous. He oddly falls in love with the ugly Socrates and "He tried what? To make Socrates, we will say, manifest his desire to him because he knows that Socrates desires him; what he wanted was a sign" (Ibid, p.116). Socrates never gave this sign. He refused to manifest his desire in any form of demand, especially sexual craving. All he agreed to do was to kindle Alcibiades' desire in dialogue, creating the paradigmatic analytic positioning for all times.

The Symbolic means of therapy are such that Imaginary certainties and constructions are given up in favor of truth. Truth is defined by Lacan in a very complex way:

> I might as well be categorical. In psychoanalytic anamnesis, it is not a question of reality, but of truth, because the effect of full speech is to reorder past contingencies by conferring upon them the sense of necessities to come, such as they are constituted by the little freedom through which the subject makes them present.
>
> (Lacan 1967, p.213)

Such discursive appropriation of personal history is the pivotal act of subjecthood. It sustains the subject in language and renders him the "scene-shifter, or even the director of the entire imaginary capture of which he would otherwise be nothing more than the living marionette" (Ibid, p.532). The precedence of the word (language) in the constitution of subjectivity allows the creative function of the analysand's speech to recreate himself according to *his* vision of himself, in terms of future possibilities rather than past contingencies.

The workings of structural principles of signification are powerful in analytic discourse. Re-ordering past contingencies does not mean controlling factual events or exposing a hidden history. Everything the analysand does is within the purview of the signifier. He can position at the epicenter of biographical signification; he can be the author of signifiers rather than their consequence. Things may no longer happen to him. He may exercise his agency and desire, and learn their potential for personal transformation in both past and future events. This would amount to 'murdering' the child that others had imagined us to be (Laplanche 1992), in favor of the child we could have been and may still be.

7.4 Free association and free-floating attention

Lacan takes Freud's initial formulation of analysis's fundamental rules in a literal, radical way. The patient must speak freely and the analyst must refrain from conceptualizing what she hears. The analyst's main task *is not to disturb the analysand's speech and not to direct it*. She needs to be silent. Not make an effort to understand. If she has an insight, she should refrain from saying so, because understanding and empathy are Imaginary and flatten or kill the patient's speech. An analyst needs to train herself not to understand. This is a matter of mental positioning: We all can stand in awe of even the simplest event. This is the ability the analyst should exercise in listening to her patient, thus optimizing the chance that the analysand's speech will express his demand and reveal his desire.

In Plato's *The Symposium*, Alcibiades speaks of Socrates 'playing the fool', despite the precious ideas he holds in his head (agalma/*objet a*). This is exactly what Lacan recommends for the analyst: 'play dead', 'play the dummy'. It will not subtract an inch of the analyst's position as the subject-supposed-to-know. Socrates showed people that *they do not know*, he showed them their lack, resonating the Lacanian analytic objective: "to isolate oneself with another to teach him what? What he is lacking! … what he is lacking is going to be learned by him as a lover" (Lacan 1960–1961). Moreover, like in analysis, for Socrates people exercise their desire in *dialogue* and that, in and of itself, is a manifestation of truth.

7.5 The cut, the void and the absence of certainty

Analysis transforms (Imaginary) certainty into the void-like shape of a question. This "… constitutes the emergence of truth in the real" (Ibid, pp.48–9). Truth is a frightening thing: "[N]othing is to be feared more than saying something that might be true" (Lacan 1967, p.525). First, because truth distances the subject from his reliance on the Other. The subject has long lived in the certainties of Imaginary and Symbolic otherness, be they a parent's will or a social convention. When the unconscious Other interferes with the ego's speech, the analysand is startled, disowning his blunder or looking to his analyst for explanation. But the analyst won't go for any of these. Instead, she terminates the session, leaving the patient high and dry, like Socrates did with Alcibiades. In this manner, she forces the analysand to ponder the enigmatic signifier that had surfaced from the unconscious. At that moment, the analysand is alone with his truth, with no external rules to turn to. Every such 'cut' is an encounter with the authenticity of the Real, with gaps and voids that underline the arbitrariness of representation in both the Imaginary and the Symbolic. When the analysand eventually signifies the event, he will also experience the après coup nature of signification.

7.6 Identifying master signifiers

The analyst listens for the demands that inhibit both speech and desire, expressing a repressed psychic economy. These demands appear in the form of signifiers-of-old, as master signifiers of sorts, in the same way that the name-of-the-father does: Foreclosing some signifiers while necessitating others. Such demands determine what may be thought and said. In themselves, master signifiers carry no inherent signification, only implicit references to the desire of others. Despite appearing often enough, they carry no clear meanings. A patient may say: 'This comes from being brought up on Park Avenue'. We realize that this determines him in various ways, but it is often amazing how the analysand himself can't explain what he means – what does it entail or disallow, being brought up on Park Avenue? It is like trying to describe the necessary conditions of being 'human' – what are they? Having a body? A soul? Being moral? Responsible? What do these words mean anyway? Are they perhaps just as abstruse as the signifiers they come to replace?

The analytic task is to identify these signifiers, question them, strip them of obvious, contingent meanings. Doing this often unmoors the experience of identity. The analysand may then realize that he has been worshiping contingent shrines. He may learn that submitting himself to the demands of others is a cover-up for not knowing what he wants. There is no godly truth, desire or demand to guide him. Socrates "wreaks havoc everywhere simply by ... telling little stories which seem to be about everyday affairs ..." (Miller 1997). But these 'little stories' shook up the listener's identity, unmoored his certainty and unsettled accepted truisms. Socrates freed desire and undermined authority, for which he was put to death by the controlling machinery of the state.

7.7 The analytic objective: Traversing of the fantasy

The analyst, as subject-supposed-to-know, is positioned as an ideal. She refuses this position by, say, asking questions and skirting the world of demand, which brings out the analysand's encounter with void and lack (of self and other). In this way, analysis undermines the promise and ideal of the fundamental fantasy and frees from its bonds and limits. The fantasy and the subject-supposed-to-know fall together. In Seminar 15, Lacan (1967–1968) illustriously describes the fall of the subject-supposed-to-know. The tenure of her superior position eventually ends, like those of the former guises of *objet a* – the placenta, the breast and the stool. After the pass (see below), the analysand knows "what his analyst has become in the accomplishment of this act, namely, this residue, this rubbish, this rejected thing" (Ibid, p.70). The analyst (and all others) loses her position as holder of *objet a*. The subject now assumes *objet a* as lack.

The pass, instituted in 1967, is the formal ceremony of passage from candidacy to membership in Lacanian psychoanalytic societies. The candidate receives her formal qualification and ends her analytic training. She appears before her institute and describes the fall of her fantasy. She must recognize the essential lack in self and other by acknowledging as vital the impossibility of sustaining the fantasy's illusions of perfection. The pass removes the enormous, alienating burden of the ego ideal and releases the subject from relentless pursuit of the unattainable *objet a*. She acknowledges the pain and destitution of being orphaned and accepts responsibility and freedom of choice. Freedom from the demand of the Other also frees desire and identity.

7.8 The passage from discourse to act, from knowledge to know-how

In Seminar 8 (Lacan 1960–1961), *objet a* as lack is represented in the chain of signifiers, i.e. in the way the subject chooses to inscribe himself in discourse *according to his own desire*. In Seminar 15 (Lacan 1967–1968), the acceptance of lack requires an *act* and the traversing of the fantasy becomes 'a *passage a l'acte*'

(Ibid, p.20). Lacan's subject is now *more* than an infinite slippage in the Symbolic; more than a director of scenes. He is now an *actor*. The whole realm of action opens as *possibility* at the end of analysis including, among other things, a voluntary arrest in this slippage through an act of agency. In the words of the late Wittgenstein: "The real discovery is the one that enables me to stop philosophizing when I want to …" (Wittgenstein 1953, p1s133).

Lacan gives a beautiful example of what may constitute an act: "… If I walk up and down here while speaking to you, that does not constitute an act, but if one day it is to cross a certain threshold by which I put myself outside the law, that day my motor activity will have the value of an act" (Lacan 1967–1968, p.5). Simply put, an **act** entails challenging the name-of-the-father (the law) as its determining factor. This leads us in the direction of conceiving of the subject as *she who appears when resisting the Other*.

Related to this is also the difference between knowledge ('savoir') and know-how ('savoir-faire', art of living). The fall of the subject-supposed-to-know leads to the collapse of knowledge as an idealized category.[2] In its stead, a know-how appears that links to action and agency, which constitute the subject as causing effects in the Other. Know-how, resonating Heidegger's Aletheia, "can emerge at any moment" (Ibid). It is an *event*. It disappears and reappears, guiding you in working out *something*, in this case, something that defines who you are and how you choose to live your life. It is operational knowledge that cannot be formulated or appear in petrified form.

This amounts to a whole theory of the subject's freedom, choice, and responsibility: An ethics. We re-emphasize what a paradigm shift this is for someone whose life and identity had been determined and guided by others. Hereon, there is no one to look up to, blame or hide from. Guilt, which constitutes neurotic existence and attaches to transgression in relation to an Other, unveils itself here as a strategy of instating a demanding Other and relinquishing one's own desire. Take for example feeling guilty at being late. This immediately implicates an anticipating Other whom, one imagines, is waiting for me and is terribly disappointed that I don't appear at the prescribed time. The 'assuming' of my desire involves the fall not only of my analyst, but also of all those others who act as directors of my life. Understanding that they do not exist may radically free me of their demands and restriction, of my guilt. Yet, this comes at a price: I realize I am alone, I am no longer a child. There are no big Others around to terrorize me or take care of me. *Their fall is the end of my imagined childhood, it is the beginning of my life as an orphan and a subject of existential freedom.* This seems to draw us closer to both life and death.

7.9 The anchoring of a new identity

Lacan's career and his notions of therapeutic achievement centered on the subversion of the subject and her Other. Having achieved that, he sets out to destabilize further the Symbolic hegemony over individual life and to seek new anchorage for the subject's identity. He sought an energetic force that could be mobilized for the task, a force that was relatively free of the authority of the law. This may be described as Lacan's 'turn' in his final seminars: From the subject of (Symbolic) desire to the subject of (Real) jouissance. Lack ceased to be a lone ideal and Lacan began to discuss satisfaction.

Formerly, the Other of jouissance, desire, was investigated and valorized. Jouissance was avoided more than explored. That makes sense, being intimately tied up with what Lacan understood as the death drive. Hereon, satisfaction did not depend anymore on the free and dynamic movement of desire. Instead it involved the know-how of living and experiencing jouissance. In the logic of Symbolic reasoning, this had to be *unconscious*, which located jouissance on a different order. Lacan realized he had to introduce the Real as a dimension of the unconscious and explain its manifestations in terms of jouissance. Jouissance now received its full dimension as experiencing the Real through the body. This introduced a being in itself, a Das Ding, that seeks nothing external. It was outside of the law, impossible to articulate and unlimited. A **primal, mythic jouissance** that, after castration, was limited and only "… reached on the inverse scale of the Law of desire" (Lacan 1967, p.700). This was surplus jouissance, by contrast to *phallic jouissance* ('of the limb'), which was *partial and misleading, as it promised complementarity between the sexes.* Phallic jouissance functioned within the confines of the name-of-the-father and its law. The third form of jouissance, which Lacan called *feminine*, lay *beyond* the signifier. It existed outside the rules and regulations of Symbolic law, freeing itself progressively from the reign of linguistic meaning. It disregarded conformity and the demand of articulation, delving into a kind of bodily experience that was unknown, radically original and mystic. Feminine jouissance marked the possibilities of replacing the name-of-the-father (lawful order) with a different signifier, S(A̶).

The character of post-phallic jouissance can be illuminated by two binaries: Truth and knowledge; thinking and being. Lacan's initial emphasis on the Symbolic set some store on knowledge and rule-governed psychic activity. Throughout his writings, Lacan progressively undermined knowledge and thought ("I think where I am not, therefore I am where I do not think" (Lacan 1967, p.430)) and began offering truth through increasingly vague definitions, until it becomes *a mode of being* (divorced from knowledge and thought). Both truth and being were integrated into the Real. The flashes of their manifestation became both contingent and highly particular. Feminine jouissance anchored them in radically different ways of thinking, knowing and existing. It allowed the subject the freedom from complete subjection to the Other.

What cannot be fully inscribed in the realm of the law and the signifier is "the path of ex-sistence", characterized by a "jouissance one experiences and yet knows nothing about" (Lacan 1972–1973, p.77). Thus, a link was formed between the feminine, being and jouissance, all highly particular and not encompassed in the law. Instead they inhabit the Real, which "… can only be inscribed on the basis of an impasse of formalization" (Ibid, p.93). Lacan created here a link between the twilight zone of the pre-Symbolic and the enlightenment of the post-Symbolic: at the center of both lie the unknown body and the experience of jouissance.

Alongside the new formulations of jouissance, as Soler (1995) explained beautifully, a new dimension of the unconscious was developed. Hitherto, the Lacanian unconscious was conceived in linguistic terms such as *the discourse of the other* or being *structured like a language*. In the 1970s, the Real dimension of the unconscious emerged: "The Real, I will say, is the mystery of the speaking body, the mystery of the unconscious" (Lacan 1972–1973, p.131). The 'mystery of the speaking body' is jouissance, the mode in which the body experiences itself, and this mode became increasingly related to the unconscious. At the same time as the linguistic unconscious began to give way to jouissance, the *Other* – as an anchor of identity – gave way to the *body.* Until now the subject we knew had twice been alienated from his bodily experiencing. First, when identifying with the mirror image and second, when accepting the distortions of Symbolic demand. We come now to re-find a particular and highly unmodified bodily dimension in the innermost being of this subject. This might be the true return to Freud.

In Seminar 23, Lacan (1974–1975, p.147) describes the Real dimension of the unconscious as arising "from the copulation of language with our own body". This 'copulation' is a bodily event, recorded in the corporeal code of jouissance. It is a primal encounter between language and body, a particular meeting between phonemic voice and phonetic flesh: The sound, rhythm and lallation of speech as other. '**Lalangue**', as Lacan called it (Ibid), is distinct from both Imaginary fantasy and formal language: It is a "knowledge articulated by dint of *lalangue,* the body that speaks there only being held together by the Real it enjoys" (Lacan 1975). What holds the body together is neither an outline (like the mirror image) nor a social convention, but rather the Real jouissance of lalangue, the music of speech, the rhyming and breathing we meet long before we understand what our parents are telling us. As babies, we respond to lalangue in very specific ways. We turn our heads, smile or cry, synchronize its rhythms or release our tension. The contingent encounter between speaking and spoken bodies creates patterns of jouissance that are very particular to the corporeality of the subjects involved. The know-how of these patterns is inscribed in the Real unconscious.

Lalangue precedes both meaning and the distinction between signifier and signified. Its elements are not signifiers; they are 'letters' that inscribe the way the subject is affected by the materiality of language. They do not require difference in order to function and act outside of chains. They are autonomous and behave more like objects than representations. The manner in which they effect jouissance is unmediated. Letters emerge in dreams and slips of the tongue. They inhabit the senseless *core* of the symptom, reminding us of Freud's idea that the symptom is a source of satisfaction. In Lacan's words, the symptom is "the way in which each one enjoys the unconscious insofar as the unconscious determines it" (Lacan 1974–1975, p.111). The core of the symptom holds a unique knowledge-without-a-subject, a particular operational knowledge of the ways in which jouissance needs to be handled.

Experienced on the level of the speaking (and spoken-to) body, jouissance reanimates the Real body as organism, lost to the Symbolic. *While the signifier alienates the organic body, jouissance evokes it*, but at a price: It dissolves the subject's bond with the Other and renders it replaceable. The Symbolic and the Real modes of subjecthood embody different existential equations: In the former, the *subject* is distinct from her body and metonymically glides along a signifying chain; in the latter, the subject is inseparable from a body, marked by a letter that moors and holds jouissance.

Both Freud and Lacan construe the analytic work as freeing arrested desires by understanding the encoded message of the symptom. This often mitigates the symptom's effect, but rarely eliminates it. Just like in dreams, every symptom retains an unrelenting core, a reservoir of pleasure and pain that does not answer to meaning and signification. As Soler construes it (1995), this core holds the letter, the bodily inscription, of the way a particular mother's language affected the particular enjoying and pained body of her child. Acknowledging this 'pure' part of the symptom and acquiring the know-how of its assimilation into the subject's life amounts to mastering the knowledge of the Real unconscious. In Lacan's formulations of the subject of jouissance, this acknowledgement heralds the final phase of analysis. Henceforth, its acceptance signals the subject's singularity, implying the assimilation of the parts of himself that will forever retain their alterity in relation to the Symbolic.

What the subject gains in analysis is the ability to exercise choice. Whereas formerly he established identity by Symbolic means, conforming with the Other's demand, analysis allows him to identify himself in the *body* as Other. This bodily identity is wholly his own and answers the particular terms of his personal economy of jouissance. Having recourse to core jouissance transforms the symptom into a 'sinthome': it introduces a subject where there once was a void. This implies that the body now replaces the name-of-the-father in binding together the three orders (Symbolic, Imaginary and Real). The sinthome allows the subject to discover and formulate his secret, his private name. It is the "equivalent of the Real" (Lacan 1974–1975, p.120) and anchors the subject in his body rather than in the Other. It embodies a singularity that doesn't conform. On the whole, the sinthome stands in relation to symptom like the letter stands in relation to the signifier.

The sinthome underlines the manner in which analysis is a process of *feminization*. Lacan writes: "Analytic experience encounters its terminus (terme) here, for the only thing it can produce, according to my writing (gramme), is ... this signifier, S1 as the signifier of ... the idiot's jouissance" (Lacan 1972–1973, p.94). Analysis unveils the arbitrary, contingent and senseless basis of our being inasmuch as it involves a master-signifier. It signifies nothing. In Seminar 5 Lacan writes that if the phallus ever reveals itself, it will be seen as nothing but a signifier, devoid of any inherent potency. The phallus creates a coherent universe by granting Oedipal imperatives their superior status. Dubbing it 'idiotic' traverses the Oedipal backbone of society and the associated illusions. It deconstructs normative heterosexuality and undermines its coercive power.

This normative universe might be enough for the man, but a woman exceeds it. Through her relation to S(A̸), she gives her name to desire, marks its trajectory and determines her own identity. She may adopt any name, her own included, to bind the orders that connect her desire to a lawful universe. *This* law will be of her own making. What we see here is an equivalence between feminization and the processes of creating a sinthome. By replacing the master signifier with one of our choosing, we reclaim both desire and jouissance as an anchoring of identity. This frees us from the domination of the Other. It also plants us, or rather – replants us – in our body as a source of polymorphous pains and pleasures.

For Lacan, James Joyce is an example of someone who gave his own 'name' to a totally particular way of binding the orders. For example, he creates a stable structure that binds the Symbolic and the Real, but renders the Imaginary superfluous. He did this by giving us full access to the materiality of the letter while, at the same time, preserving the English syntax without creating any Imaginary meaning. The reader can enjoy the text without being able to imagine a storyline. It is clear that Lacanian analysis shares this ideal (Soler 1995), but how can we do this with daily, ordinary language?

We do not present this question in order to answer it, but rather in order to return to original wonders. Freud discovered that symbolic meanings are inscribed on the flesh. Lacan capitalized on the effects of the Symbolic to decompose or change them. This is the consequence of creating the effects of the Symbolic in the Real. Something happens during therapy. Different psychoanalytic thinkers attribute change to different mechanisms of the psyche, but all agree that there is an effect. The rest is conjecture. The sinthome may be one of these effects, where self-knowledge is gained with similar tools. For years we listen to someone, someone listens to us. Gradually, the sinthome emerges as a know-how that is not on the side of the Symbolic, because the analytic relation is never *only* Symbolic. We exist within it with our bodies, with our ways of enjoying our speech and our symptoms, and we negotiate with an Other who offers herself to help us relinquish the command of the superego: Enjoy! Our bodies create a tempo, a music, a coordinated movement that comes together to a know-how of being and suffering. They command intense pleasures in ways that we had never experienced before. We consequently gain a kind of knowledge that cannot be articulated, taught or transferred, only experienced and co-created, as a way of analytic being.

Notes

1 The gap between the subject of the statement and the subject of enunciation comes out very powerfully in sentences such as 'I am dead'. Clearly, the statement could not be enunciated if its subject were dead.
2 Lacan never set much store on knowledge. Indeed, he often underlined its Imaginary character and tendency to obstruct desire.

Chapter 8

The Political Subject

The Lacanian subject is literally *of* society, *of* politics. She is shaped by the arbitrary terms of the Other's order. It is the stuff from which she is made. At the same time, the Other defines her main challenge: In her quest to know and assume her desire, the subject must learn her particularity and navigate within the socio-political fabric that constituted her. This particularity, by definition, entails divergence from the ways and forms of the o/Other. Trying to hold both ends of the stick, Lacan created a psychoanalytic theory in which psychic change involves resisting the Other, eluding his grasp and transgressing the norms. This renders political any intrapsychic change.

8.1 The notion of discourse

'The Other side of psychoanalysis' (Lacan 1969–1970), where the notion of 'discourse' is developed, was written after the students' revolts of 1968. It discusses issues that extend classical psychoanalysis and the perspective of the individual, and addresses the structure of social bonds. Lacan introduced four discourses that are *social, intersubjective constructs that hold the subject and subjecthood at their epicenter.* Subjecthood is what distinguishes 'discourse' from 'language': The former always relates to subjecthood, while the latter is a formal system.

Each of the four discourses describes a unique fundamental relationship that gives rise to a particular social bond. The **master's discourse** relates to rules and laws that govern various social bodies. This lawful system derives from, and accords with, one main,

DOI: 10.4324/9781003106883-8

masterful principle. The **university discourse** refers to socially recognized systems of knowledge studied or investigated in academic institutions. The **analyst's discourse** encompasses the speech with which the analyst/other, acting as *objet petit a*, addresses the speech of the divided subject. Finally, the **hysteric's discourse** refers to the subversive ways of articulating the questions 'Who am I?' and 'Who are you in relation to me?'. It is clear from their modes of creation that additional forms of discourse may be thought of.

8.2 The four positions and terms

The structure of discourse is comprised of four different compartments representing four discursive *positions* that stand in a fixed relationship to each other (Figure 8.1). The first and second positions in the upper line are self-evident in the sense of requiring a speaker, an agent of speech, and an addressed other. The arrow between them depicts the direction of communication and implicates a controlling function. This relation "indicated here with an arrow, a direction, is always defined as impossible" (Ibid, p.258). True to Lacanian thought, as depicted also in Schema L, the first fact of communication is given in its inevitable failure.

The result of the speech act, the *product*, appears in the next position when moving clockwise (right side of the lower line). On the left lower side of the diagram we have *truth*, where the psychoanalytic perspective becomes a *discourse*. Logically, truth is not the fourth but the first position in the sequence of speech. Its position under the agent comes to show that truth drives communication, acting as a starting position for speech, even when unconscious and therefore unknown to the agent.

Now, truth is probably the trickiest element in speech and forms a major part in its failure. Lacan thought that truth and speech

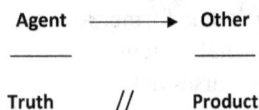

$$\begin{array}{ccc} \textbf{Agent} & \longrightarrow & \textbf{Other} \\[4pt] \underline{\quad} & & \underline{\quad} \\[4pt] \textbf{Truth} & // & \textbf{Product} \end{array}$$

Figure 8.1 The positions

are inherently incompatible. "Do not place your trust in the truth, it has a relationship to what? Not to knowledge certainly but precisely to this Real ... This indeed is the reason why it can only be expressed in a half-saying" (Ibid, p.244). Since truth is Real, it cannot be known or expressed by Symbolic means. At best it is 'half-said' and cannot appear in the product of communication. Lacan puts this strongly: "Production, in any case has no relationship with the truth" (Ibid, p.258). This is the element of impossibility that ensures the failure of communication and explains why no arrow exists on the lower line. Not only does communication fail, there is something that blocks it: The radical disjunction between discourse's *truth* and its *product*.

On the whole, these categories express the basic conundrum of Symbolic subjecthood. Part of the Symbolic subject always belies him, both through his repressions and by virtue of those parts of himself that are of the Real. This subject will represent himself as a signifier to another signifier/subject through signifiers that will always only 'refer', and point in the direction of an unknowable truth. What we have here is not only the subject's divided nature. We also have the radical disjunction of the Symbolic and the Real.

Thus, what we know of discourse through this initial formalization is that it is going to fail. Each of the four discourses demonstrates a certain desire and its failure, resulting in a typical social bond. But this, of course, is also the cause of perpetuation in both speech and discourse. We continue talking because we have not gotten ourselves across. Were we to understand ourselves or be understood by others, we would lack both inner and outer motivation to speak. However, we also continue speaking because speech organizes us on collective levels. One might say that social organization is represented in discourse in a way that parallels the representation of the divided subject in the signifier. This keeps the wheels of discourse turning, but they do so for another reason, which Lacan described by referring to Marx's political economy.

In Marx's theory, the production and circulation of commodities is driven by need and demand in a manner that parallels that of desire and jouissance. In addition to need and demand, there is always a gap between the reified value of past work and the living value of transforming work. Marx calls this gap 'surplus value'.

Lacan offers an analogy to this dynamic power of economic circulation in terms of desire and jouissance. In Phallic and Symbolic dynamics, there is always an equilibrium between desire and jouissance. The Real upsets this equilibrium and the imbalance produces a 'surplus jouissance' that keeps discourse going, circulating.

The above positions may account for mental economy, but do not suffice to create the four discourses. To do this, Lacan summons four familiar terms: S1, S2, $\mathcal{S}$ and a. S1 is the master signifier of old, the symbolic element the subject had identified with in parting from the mother. Recall that S1 carries no inherent meaning yet serves as a 'quilting point' (*point de capiton*), halting and stabilizing the endless play of signifiers by organizing affect and knowledge. S2 represents the *chains of signifiers* that follow the law of the master signifier. Through semiotic combination (metonymy/displacement and metaphor/substitution) they create structured systems of knowledge (*savoir*). $\mathcal{S}$, the third term is the divided, barred subject of the Symbolic. The last of the terms is the lost object, the *objet a*, the basis of all mental causality, the cause and final term of desire. All discourses retain the serial order of the terms while their *positions* change. Each discourse is created by a clockwise, quarter rotation of terms between positions (see Figure 8.2).

8.3 The master's discourse

The master's discourse (Figure 8.2) describes the initial positioning of the subject in the Symbolic order and also alludes to the Hegelian metaphor of master and slave. The agent of discourse here is the master signifier that addresses and organizes all other signifiers, appearing in the Other position as S2. The product of

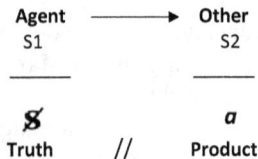

Agent	⟶	Other
S1		S2
——		——
$\mathcal{S}$		a
Truth	//	Product

Figure 8.2 The master's discourse

this discourse is that which is inevitably lost in signification: the *objet a*. The truth of this situation is given in the nature of the divided subject.

On a social level, this discourse first appeared when monarchy displaced 'natural' communities such as family and tribe. These early organizations were pre-Symbolic, based on needs rather than on arbitrary rules. The monarch, by contrast, is arbitrarily granted absolute power that need not make sense or provide justification. The *meaning* of the monarch's reign is his *ability* to reign, regardless of content. This parallels the phallus's position in that it carries no meaning yet holds the key to organizing all other signifiers. The monarch also controls all forms of knowledge in a manner that conceals any lack, but error and political subversion still exist and forfeit perfection.

The master's discourse implies the directionality of power relations, as indicated by the arrow. The master/S1 controls all signifiers/subjects but, as we remember, this may be entirely devoid of content. As Lacan writes: "A real Master, ... desires to know nothing at all, he wants things to work" (Ibid, p.6). Imperative speech, like that of the monarch or the boss, is not so simple: "... it is in effect impossible for there to be a master who is able to make his world work. To make people work is even more exhausting than to work oneself ... The master never does it. He makes a sign, the master signifier, and everyone runs away!" This begs the question of the sign's power, and Lacan's answer, as usual, is given in negative form: "How is it that the discourse of the master holds fast? It is the other face of the function of truth, not the open face, but the dimension in which it is made necessary as a debt for something hidden" (Ibid, p.23). *Subjects need their truth*. As their truth is inherently veiled, they accept a pseudo-organizing, arbitrary axiom in its stead. Lacan is illustrating here the way the Symbolic is 'imaginarized' in the master's discourse, providing an illusion of total and coherent knowledge, posing in the absolute garb of truth. The slave not only gives way to the control of truth, but also perpetuates it, fearing its fall. Since all subjects need the big Other, we all, in a sense, submit to a monarch. This was also Lacan's warning to the unruly students – 'If you seek a master, you will find one'.

8.4 The university discourse

For Lacan, the classic master was a craftsman, while the modern master is a capitalist. They are different in the place they accord to knowledge: The craftsman produces it, while the capitalist owns it. The one who accumulates knowledge is always a 'slave' inasmuch as he is the one who engages with the world through working. But the capitalist master dispossesses the slave of his knowledge and turns it into a dictate. The slave understands that it is useless to change anything in the status of his own agency, but since knowledge answers to something the master wants, it is where his claim to agency may be realized. This is how the university discourse had been born. In capitalist society, knowledge has become the universal currency of power: It is marked by the reign of the university discourse. The status of knowledge grows to the extent that "all knowledge has shifted into the place of the master" (Ibid, p.9). This state of affairs is represented in Figure 8.3:

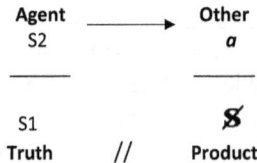

Figure 8.3 The university discourse

As can be seen, knowledge occupies the agent's position, without knowing that it is guided by an unknown master. When unknowingly determined by an arbitrary, unknown master, knowledge becomes little more than a ruse, hiding the master's existence. It actually achieves nothing but its master's interest – this time even without awareness of it. This would be resonating Horkheimer's (1972) critique of traditional 'scientific' theory that, while portraying as objective, is really guided by capitalist interests. Scientists are truly blind to being controlled, Horkheimer adds, because they themselves are products of the system whose means of power they perpetuate. Horkheimer and Lacan concur that the main products of this discourse are *the subjects of the system* (s as 'product'). And so Lacan addresses the rebelling students: "You are the products of the University ... even if only in this respect – ... that you leave here, equal more or less to credits. You have all made yourselves into credits. You leave here stamped with credits" (Lacan 1969–1970, p.26).

The social system is governed by an obfuscated, unknown, senseless and arbitrary master signifier that poses as sense and order. In Lacan's words "what affirms itself as being nothing other than knowledge ... is called, in ordinary language, *bureaucracy*" (Ibid, p.42, emphasis original). Perhaps more than any other author, Kafka's genius portrays the relentless workings of a blind, oiled and efficient machinery that holds no sense and does nothing but perpetuate itself. Lacan also calls it 'capitalism'.

By endlessly repeating its own logic, both bureaucracy and capitalism crush the agency of the subject, forcing her to conform to the machinery of which she is part and product. And repetition, curiously enough, ".... has a certain relationship with the limit of this subject and this knowledge, which is called enjoyment, jouissance" (Ibid, p.8). This is why the agent's addressee in Figure 8.3 (upper right side) is the *objet a*. University discourse tries to control *objet a*'s manifestations and the surplus jouissance it holds. The frenzy of consumerism often shows how we almost kill ourselves in order to obtain our next acquisition, driven by repetition, way beyond the afforded pleasure. Capitalism tells us what we need and desire, what grants us satisfactions. Its repetitive grip holds us in the throes of jouissance. We agonize over what car to buy, never questioning the fact of wanting a car; we compulsively search for vacation resorts without asking ourselves what vacationing may actually mean for us. We search for endless imaginary *objet a*-s that are always disappointing and we bleed for the measure of jouissance granted us in the system. We abide by the superego's command to enjoy and then overstep both it and our means.

Is there a way out here? Only the subject may be responsible for replacing the senseless S2 with truth: "[Truth] is to be produced by those who are the substitutes for the slaves of antiquity, namely, by those who are themselves products, as they say, that are just as consumable as the others" (Ibid, p.43). The only chance of subverting the course of capitalist consumerism lies in allowing the Real to shape our desire.

8.5 The analyst's discourse

In the analyst's discourse, power and influence is paradoxically accorded to the one *not* speaking, the one who listens and takes a passive position. But this passivity, this suspension of ego, is what allows the analyst to function as the analysand's *objet a*. She is in the agent's position in her function to abolish the world of demand and gradually free the analysand's desire.

In Chapter 7 we described how transference institutes the analyst as subject-supposed-to-know. The analysand is the one to attribute knowledge to the analyst according to his own needs and desires. The analyst is supposed to know in the eyes of the analysand, but in her own eyes must remember that she knows nothing. Otherwise she is not analyzing, but rather indoctrinating. And yet the knowledge attributed to the analyst is not an illusion. Only, it is the analysand's unconscious that holds the knowledge the analysand needs. But his analyst has a know-how as to how to access this knowledge. "(T)here is one thing that we are really inured to, trained in, in analytic practice, which is this business of manifest content and latent content. That is our experience. For the analysand who is there, the latent content is his knowledge. We are there to get him to know everything that he does not know even while knowing it. That is what the unconscious is" (Ibid, p.134). The analyst's training and experience allow her gradually to access both the analysand's knowledge and the element controlling it:

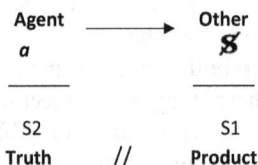

Agent	$\longrightarrow$	Other
a		$\slashed{S}$
---		---
S2		S1
Truth	//	Product

Figure 8.4 The analyst's discourse

[W]hat is remarkable is that it is on his side that there is S2,
that there is knowledge – whether he acquires this knowledge
by listening to his analysand or whether it is a knowledge that
has already been acquired, mapped out, something that at a
certain level, one can limit to analytic know-how.

(Ibid, p.46)

What is it that the analyst knows how to do? She knows how to
create the analytic product. She knows how to allow the analysand
to know what binds and subjects his desire. She knows how to make
known the analysand's master signifier – S1. In Seminar 20, Lacan
formulates the end of analysis in terms of S1 as its product: "Analytic experience encounters its terminus (terme) here, for the only thing
it can produce, according to my writing (gramme), is S1" (Lacan
1972–1973, p.178). Analysis ends when the unconscious yields its
master (S1). The master is the one who had hitherto determined the
subject's modes of perception, relation and emotion; it determined
the constraints that constricted or twisted the analysand's desire and
jouissance. The uncovering of S1 entails also knowing its senseless-
ness, its arbitrary nature: "S1 which, of all the signifiers, is the signifier for which there is no signified, and which, with respect to
meaning (sens), symbolizes the failure thereof" (Ibid, p.80). In this
process, the big Other is toppled as master of the analysand's desire
and jouissance. Hereon, the analysand is doomed to an orphan's
existence, but this is also what frees him to enjoy choice and
creativity (alongside the persisting anxieties).

There is another dimension that touches upon both the individual and the social and gives S1 an additional meaning: "...
[P]erhaps it is from the discourse of the analyst ... *that there can
emerge another style of master signifier*. In truth, whether it is
another style or not, it is not tomorrow or the day after you will
know what it is ..." (Lacan 1969–1970, p.261, our emphasis). If
we persevere with analysis, we may find in the depth of the
unconscious additional S1s. Knowing now that they are senseless,
we understand that they acquire meaning through the jouissance
involved in their compulsive repetition. Released from the
common Oedipal S1 and potential additional arbitrary S1s, there
might emerge "another style of signifier" that is wholly personal,

holding the key and code, the 'know-how' of a certain jouissance: "...
(the) key lies in the questioning of what enjoyment is about. Enjoyment is limited by natural processes. But to tell the truth, we know
nothing about these natural processes. We simply know that we have
ended up by considering as natural the mollycoddling in which a more
or less organised society maintains us, except that everyone is dying to
know what would happen if it really hurts" (Ibid).

How does this play out on the social level? Firstly, by releasing
the hold of S1, we reduce the phallocentric and paternalistic
domination on social life. This may already make for a more heterogeneous, 'queer' society, less imprisoned in binaries and granting its subjects greater freedoms of both thought and enjoyment.
Secondly, ordinary ways of thinking (paradigms) change from
time to time, but this can only happen on the basis of individual
subjects who subvert S1 and, with it, the reign of the name-of-the-
father. This involves extended individuality and diversity across all
levels of cultural life. It implies greater acceptance of ex-centricity
and probably greater creativity.

In 1964, Lacan began a seminar titled 'The Names of the Father'.
The title already gives away the main idea of what is hinted at in
Seminar 17 and plainly stated in Seminar 20: That there are a mul-
titude of S1s and, with that, a plurality of languages within each and
every language. This means that identification with the father may
not be the last word in the development of the Oedipal complex. The
figure of the father then ceases to be the epitome of subjectivity and
culture, but rather becomes a symptom and an instrument.[1] It is an
interesting irony that, in 1964, the International Psychoanalytic
Association agreed to grant membership to the Société Française de
Psychanalyse (Lacan's psychoanalytic society) on condition that
Lacan himself be stripped of his status as a training analyst. Lacan
then founded his new school, L'École Freudienne de Paris. *This is a
real-life example of rejecting S1, paying the price, and binding the
orders with one's own name.*

8.6 The hysteric's discourse

The last rotation of terms creates the hysteric's discourse, construed by Lacan as the objective of psychoanalysis: "What the

```
       Agent    ─────────▶    Other
         ₷                     S1
       ───────               ───────


         a                     S2
       Truth       //        Product
```

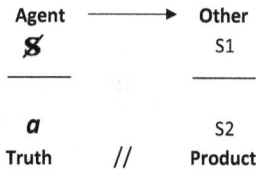

Figure 8.5 The hysteric's discourse

analyst sets up as an analytic experience can be simply put – it is the hysterisation of discourse … the structural introduction, under artificial conditions, of the discourse of the Hysteric" (Ibid, p.44). Here, the hysteric (₷) addresses the master signifier, S1, and the divided subject of the unconscious challenges the master signifier. Inasmuch as ₷ is feminine and S1 masculine, we also have here a challenge of the phallocentric, paternalistic dimension of the Symbolic order. As Caquot notes in his dialogue with Lacan, referring to the Hebrew of husband and wife: "Even though Baal [husband] is the master. We can observe that the feminine, Beoula ['husbended'], is the woman as husband in potency" (Ibid, p.203). In other words, it is the owner of the symptom creating a situation in which "… the law (is) being called into question as a symptom" (Ibid, p.55).

   The question at stake here (borrowing a Lacanian phrase) is the interpretation of the relations between the hysteric, the master and the *objet a*: Is the hysteric again the symptom of the man in the sense that she is his object? Or is she the standing proof "… that language cannot cope with the breadth of what she as a woman can open up about enjoyment" (Ibid, p.68)? If we see the symptom's core as what holds a bit of Real jouissance, these two interpretative possibilities become compatible. In fact, what we understand is that hysteric discourse can bring us as close to the Real as we can get.

   The hysteric wants a master.

      That is absolutely clear. This is so even to the point that the question must be asked if it is not from this that the invention of the discourse of the Master started … She wants the other to be a master, to know many things, but all the same not to know enough ... In other words, she wants a master over whom she reigns ... this is not necessarily specific to one sex. As soon as you ask the question 'What does so-and-so want?' you enter into the function of desire, and you bring out the master-signifier.

(Lacan 1969–1970, p.153)

This means that the hysteric has overturned the master and his reign. What she is left with is the truth of her desire and with knowledge that will never exhaust this truth: "What leads to knowledge is the hysteric's discourse" (Ibid, p.18). She solicits knowledge by offering herself as its precious object, compelling the male (phallic marker) to generate more of it. But, on the other hand, she pushes knowledge to its limits, eventually demonstrating that it does not and cannot coincide with the truth.

Knowledge fails to supply the hysteric with an answer to the question of who she is. All answers fail to master their object; none can silence the hysteric. This failure of knowledge incessantly fuels the continuation of analysis. In this respect, what potentially lies at the horizon of the hysteric is accepting herself as open-ended and 'unanswered', i.e., assuming her own lack. What had begun with the 'truth' of placing herself as object of desire, animating the analyst in ways that cause him to create knowledge, ends with the truth of lack, of pure desire. This is the first time that term (*a*) and position (truth) align themselves with the overall nature of the human condition: Both truth and lack are of the Real.

8.7 The role of psychoanalysis in political discourse

In Seminar 17 Lacan defines social configurations, mapping out their origin, logic and method of perpetuation. Lacan 'un-imaginarizes' these dynamics, lays bare their mechanisms and thus allows their deconstruction. The subject as a socio-linguistic being necessarily partakes in (at least one) discourse, though not necessarily as agent. This grants her an a priori political positioning. She is always part of social bonds and organizations, whether in the position of agent, product or mastered other. She therefore always bears responsibility for these bonds and her position within them. For example, in the master's discourse, one may participate in legislation, be an obedient citizen or a transgressor, etc. In a similar manner, one may 'fall in' with academic life in the university discourse or comment about it, even retell it (e.g., David Lodge 1984). All-in-all, subjects can be characterized socially according to their various positions in the different discourses.

Being a political subject, being part of the fabric of politics, does not yet imply being a political *agent*. Political agency requires action, begging the question of what would qualify as such. Clear, unequivocal political action would dwell in an act that knowingly and intentionally violates certain laws or norms and reflects the desire to change the law. For example, stealing apples from the grocery may pass as a political action if it is accompanied by a radical critique of private property (Stavrakakis 1999). Clearly, organized action forms the paradigmatic instance of political action but, for Lacan, the discourses of the analyst and the hysteric both include an inherent political element.

The *analyst's discourse* renders the subject aware of Symbolic rules. It uncovers S1, thus effectually revealing the fundamentals of power structures. This offers the first step towards unsettling the prevalent strategies of political and social control. In the terms of critical theory, *the hysteric's discourse* may emancipate scientific discourse by dethroning its masters, allowing knowledge both its limitations and the mystery of its infinite production (Wajcman 2003). The hysteric's desire is a perpetuating force: she is always a question. Any answer given, any additional 'thing', is lost, recreating the *objet a* and its driving force. Spoken signification can only half state the truth, creating the disjunction that must be acknowledged: Knowledge and truth do not coincide. What we gain here is that no master may persist and knowledge cannot be monopolized. Truth is always, only, of the Real.

Analysis always addresses both other and Other, both personal and collective otherness. The latter is always political in one way or another. This truth about analysis unsettles Marx's 11th thesis on Feuerbach, whereby philosophers have only interpreted the world and the thing is to change it (Marx 1888). In analysis, utterance is action. This is a general truth, but it is particularly poignant regarding Lacanian analysis because of the emphasis on (and awareness of) the Real. The disclosure of the Real, in itself, is always a political event. The Real will forever reveal that the Symbolic is arbitrary and carries no inherent meaning, thus undermining it, pulling the metaphysical carpet from under its feet. In Lacan's aphoristic expression, there is no other of the Other.

Note

1   These ideas are explicitly stated in Seminar 23 (Lacan 1975–1976) but may be said to have already existed implicitly in Lacan's thought ever since posing the question of a possible treatment to psychosis.

Epilogue

We hope that, through our retelling of the Lacanian story, we have addressed the opening questions of this book's Preface. In our closing comments, we wish to re-(ad)dress some of them, starting with the need for another introduction to Lacanian psychoanalysis. One of Lacan's well-known aphorisms says that certain things never stop being written. These things tie up with what defines us as human, which is often experienced as an encounter with something that has always already been there, in and around us. In Lacanian psychoanalysis, these 'things' revolve around the event of speaking and listening to an other. Whether it involves language or lalangue, this event is transformative and has the power utterly to make us up.

Lacan often claimed that he only offered a re-reading of Freudian ideas. Indeed, in one of his last public appearances, when his reputation was already spreading in widening intellectual and artistic circles beyond psychoanalysis, he said that he knows that some psychoanalysts identify themselves as Lacanian, but he never considered himself as anything other than Freudian. We would not dismiss this statement as merely stylistic. Freud was the original landmark and lighthouse of a great cultural development: Psychoanalysis and the talking cure. He defined the unconscious, the drive and the ability to create effects by means of speech. In calling himself 'Freudian', Lacan showed respect for this, as he did generally for the history of ideas. He also underlined and elaborated the centrality, dynamics and interconnections of the unconscious, sexuality and language as systems that direct the subject

DOI: 10.4324/9781003106883-9

towards the other, all of which he felt were downplayed in the Ego psychology that was prevalent in his time. And there is something more personal in his reference to Freud.

Lacan sent Freud a copy of his doctoral dissertation. Freud approved its receipt but failed to be impressed. In 1936, Lacan presented an early version of his paper on the mirror stage to the IPA's annual meeting. Ernest Jones, who chaired the session, stopped the talk for running overtime. Lacan left the event in anger, tore up the original paper and went to watch the Olympic Games. Failing again to draw the Freudian community's attention, Lacan gave up on institutional psychoanalysis and immersed himself instead in Chinese language and culture. When he returned to the psychoanalytic scene after WW2, he already had in mind the idea of running his own show. The 1950s witnessed a blooming Lacan, as he began his renowned weekly seminars at the Sainte-Anne University Hospital. These ran on for three decades and quickly became an intellectual event in Paris, a hothouse for thinking and debating psychoanalytic ideas in their widest implications. The seminars were attended by many renowned persons. In 1964, Levi-Strauss and Althusser initiated the seminars' move to Paris's most reputable academic institution, the École Normale Supérieure. This boosted Lacan's reputation and reflected the esteem he merited in the thinking community (unlike in the IPA). In 1966, the first collection of his writings – the *Écrits* – was published, but it was only in the mid-1970s that his writings were translated into English, introducing Lacan to the non-Francophile intelligentsia.

Lacan stands out as an extraordinarily original and erudite post-Freudian thinker. His writings engage with philosophy, art, literature and linguistics while, at the same time, also inspiring them. He was the first to re-inscribe the psychoanalytic subject in postmodern epistemology with such radical emphasis on otherness as the core root of subjectivity. We hope our book has given a measure of his remarkable lexical creativity. Like Zarathustra, Lacan also created a treasure of aphorisms that may be pondered upon for years: The subject-supposed-to-know; There is no such thing as a sexual relation; The woman does not exist; The unconscious is the discourse of the Other; Love is giving what one doesn't have to someone who doesn't want it; Desire is for the other's desire, etc. This wealth triggers boundless desire, a jouissance of exhausting inexhaustibility that remarkably sustains intellectual curiosity.

And yet, Lacan's influence in the English-speaking community grew slowly. This is probably due to the notorious difficulty of his writings and his rupture with the IPA (revolving especially around the changing lengths of sessions). Repeatedly rejected by the IPA, Lacan established his own institutions for both learning and training. He joined and left the SPP (the Paris Psychoanalytic Society), founded the SFP (Société Française de Psychanalyse), dismantled the SFP and started a new establishment, etc. Lacan practiced what he preached. He presented an adamant refusal to be a 'product' of institutional discourses. He despised indoctrination and was consistently subversive with regard to large truisms, his own included.

There are few formal publications of his teaching, the most notable being the *Écrits*. A large body of writings has been masterminded and edited by his son-in-law, Jacques-Alain Miller, and they had many translations which differed in wording and phrasing. Due to this, and to the complicated and rich hermeneutics of his writings, Lacanian groups kept forming and splitting, creating various Lacanian communities. This probably testifies to Lacan's breadth and intellectual agility. And yet these groups were often caught up in a sense of mission and conflict, which probably reduced their engagements with the mainstream psychoanalytic community, inspiring an impression of esoteric sectarianism.

There were also serious criticisms of the ideas of Lacan's legacy. For example, Noam Chomsky allegedly called Lacan a charlatan, claiming that his ideas contributed little to the understanding of language or linguistic behavior. Alan Sokal, an American professor of physics, published a hoax article in a reputable postmodern journal arguing that quantum mechanics was merely a linguistic phenomenon. Its acceptance for publication, Sokal argued, showed that ideas inspired by Lacan's writings and continental philosophy were utterly vacuous. Without addressing the validity of the above criticisms, we mention only the needed distinction between those who dismiss Lacan as lacking in theoretical value (late-modern thinkers clearly find postmodern texts quite unpalatable) and those engaged in serious criticism of his thought. An additional line of criticism came from feminist writers, to which we have already alluded in various places in the book.

Finally, some particularly sharp critique pertains to Lacan's idiosyncratic, flamboyant and erratic conduct towards both patients and colleagues. We point the interested reader to biographies such as Roudinesco's (2014) for an elaborate description of these. When it comes to Lacan, it is often difficult to differentiate thoughtfully between rumor, slur and fact. We have not delved into these issues here, focusing on theory and on the existential plight of the Lacanian subject, which far exceeds Lacan as an Imaginary being or a specific psychoanalytic methodology. This book was written with the thought of underlining the tension, the danger, and the immeasurable wealth that may be had by assuming otherness as a nodal point. In addition, Lacanian thought may be immeasurably insightful regarding the dynamics of contemporary society, leaning as it often does toward alienation and conflict.

Lacan's originality and audacity in revising not only Freudian thought, but the very conception of the subject and language, definitely carried a startling effect. Lacan stirred waves of emotion, thought, rhetoric and critique. In some sense, it honors him to have been such a landmark of controversy. He thought that our human nature expresses itself primarily in speech and discourse which, in turn, always engages otherness in its infinite varieties. This sets a particular ethical and psychological challenge for psychoanalysis, whose task becomes that of weaving together the search for individuality with the knowledge of its impossibility. The scene of endless desire for the other requires humility in acknowledging and accepting one's lack. We believe that the importance of this challenge may enrich the pursuit of subjecthood in psychoanalysis and beyond.

References

Allen, Mary Prudence (2020). The Complementarity of Man and Woman. Catholic Diocese of Broken Bay, https://www.bbcatholic.org. au/parish-community/marriage-and-family/understanding-the-human-p erson/the-complementarity-of-man-and-woman

Anzieu, Didier (2016). *The Skin Ego*. New York and London: Routledge.

Arendt, Hannah (1963). *Eichmann in Jerusalem: A Report on the Banality of Evil*. New York: Viking Press.

Barnard, Suzanne (ed.) (2002). *Reading Seminar XX: Lacan's Major Work on Love, Knowledge, and Feminine Sexuality*. New York: State University Press.

Barthes, Roland (1972). *Mythologies*, translated by Annette Lavers. New York: Farrar, Straus and Giroux.

Bellow, Saul (1959). *Henderson the Rain King*. Harmondsworth and New York: Penguin (1983).

Bowie, Malcolm (1991). *Lacan*. Cambridge (MA): Harvard University Press.

Breuer, Joseph and Freud, Sigmund (1895). *Studies on Hysteria*. **SE2**, London: Hogarth Press. (1955).

Buber, Martin (1958). *I and Thou*. New York: Scribner.

Butler, Judith (1990). *Gender Trouble: Feminism and the Subversion of Identity*. New York: Routledge.

Butler, Judith (1993). Imitation and Gender Insubordination. In Henry Abelove, Michèle Aina Barale and David M. Halperin (eds), *The Lesbian and Gay Studies Reader*. New York and London: Routledge, pp.307–320.

Conrad, Joseph (1902). *Heart of Darkness*. London and New York: Penguin (2011).

Danziato, Leonardo (2016). From Sexual Difference to Sexuation. *Ágora*, 19:1498–1516.

Derrida, Jacques (1974). *Of Grammatology*, translated by Gayatri Chakravorty Spivak. Baltimore: Johns Hopkins University Press.

Dor, Joel (1998). *Introduction to the Reading of Lacan: The Unconscious Structured Like a Language*, translated by Susan Fairfield. New York: Other Press.

Fink, Bruce. (1995). *The Lacanian Subject: Between Language and Jouissance*. Princeton: Princeton University Press.

Foucault, Michel (1970). *The Order of Things: An Archaeology of the Human Sciences*. New York: Vantage Books.

Freud, Sigmund (1911). *Psycho-Analytic Notes on an Autobiographical Account of a Case of Paranoia*. In **SE12**. London: Hogarth Press, pp.1–82 (1956).

Freud, Sigmund (1915). *The Unconscious*. In **SE14**, London: Hogarth Press, pp.159–215 (1957).

Freud, Sigmund (1919). *A child is Being Beaten*. In **SE17**, London: Hogarth Press, pp.177–179 (1955).

Freud, Sigmund (1920). *The Psychogenesis of a Case of Female Homosexuality*. In **SE18**, London: Hogarth Press, pp.145–172 (1957).

Freud, Sigmund (1923). *The Infantile Genital Organization of the Libido*. In **SE19**, London: Hogarth Press, pp.139–146 (1959).

Freud, Sigmund (1927). *Fetishism*. In **SE21**, London: Hogarth Press, pp.147–158 (1961).

Freud, Sigmund (1930). *Civilization and its Discontents*. In **SE21**,London: Hogarth Press, pp.57–146 (1961).

Freud, Sigmund (1933). *Femininity*. In **SE22**, London: Hogarth Press, pp.112–135 (1964).

Gherovici, Patricia (2009). Lacan's Hysterization of Psychoanalysis: From Simulation to Stimulation. *Analysis: Difference*, 15:111–126.

Hadar, Uri (2013). The Benjamin Chreode. *Studies in Gender and Sexuality*, 14:16–34.

Hadar, Uri (2022). Subject and Subjecthood: From Philosophy to Psychoanalysis. In Govrin, A. and Caspi, T. (eds), *The Routledge International Handbook of Psychoanalysis and Philosophy*. London: Routledge.

Hegel, Georg Wilhelm Friedrich (1807). *The Phenomenology of Spirit*, translated by A.V. Miller. Oxford: Oxford University Press (1977).

Heidegger, Martin (1962). *Being and Time*, translated by John Macquarrie and Edward Robinson. Oxford: Blackwells (2001).

Herera, Marcos (2010). Representante-representativo, représentant-représentation, ideational representative: which one is a Freudian concept? On the translation of Vorstellungsrepräsentanz in Spanish, French and English. *International Journal of Psychoanalysis*, 91:785–809.

Horkheimer, Max (1972). *Critical Theory: Selected Essays.* Freiburg: Herder and Herder.

Jakobson, Roman (1956). The Metaphoric and Metonymic Poles. In Dirven, René and Pörings, Ralf (eds), *Metaphor and Metonymy in Comparison and Contrast.* Amsterdam: de Gruyter, pp.41–48.

Kant, Immanuel (1781). *Critique of Pure Reason,* translated by Marcus Weigelt. London: Penguin (2008).

Klein, Melanie (1946). Notes on Some Schizoid Mechanisms. *The International Journal of Psychoanalysis,* 27:99–110.

Kojève, Alexandre (1969). *Introduction to the Reading of Hegel: Lectures on the Phenomenology of Spirit,* translated by James H. Nicols. New York: Cornel University Press.

Kristeva, Julia (1982). *Powers of Horror: An Essay on Abjection.* New York: Columbia University Press.

Kristeva, Julia (1984). *Revolution in Poetic Language.* New York: Columbia University Press.

Lacan, Jacques (1949). The mirror stage as formative of the function of the I as revealed in psychoanalytic experience. In *Écrits,* translated by Bruce Fink, pp.75–81. New York: WW Norton (2006).

Lacan, Jacques (1953–1954). *The Seminar of Jacques Lacan, Book I: Freud's Papers on Technique,* translated by John Forrester. Cambridge, UK: Cambridge University Press (1988).

Lacan, Jacques (1954–1955). *The Seminar of Jacques Lacan, Book II: The Ego in Freud's Theory and in the Technique of Psychoanalysis,* translated by Sylvana Tomaselli. New York: WW Norton (1991).

Lacan, Jacques (1955–1956). *The Seminar of Jacques Lacan, Book III: The Psychoses,* translated by Russell Grigg. New York: WW Norton (1997).

Lacan, Jacques (1957–1958). *The Seminar of Jacques Lacan, Book V: Formations of the Unconscious,* translated by Cormac Gallagher. Cambridge, UK: Polity Press (2017).

Lacan, Jacques (1958). The Direction of the Treatment and the Principles of its Power. In *Écrits,* translated by Bruce Fink, pp.489–542. New York: WW Norton (2006).

Lacan, Jacques (1959–1960). *The Seminar of Jacques Lacan, Book VII: The Ethics of Psychoanalysis,* translated by Dennis Porter. London: Routledge (1992).

Lacan, Jacques (1960–1961). *The Seminar of Jacques Lacan, Book VIII: Transference,* translated by Cormac Gallagher. www.lacaninireland.com (2011).

Lacan, Jacques (1961–1962). *The Seminar of Jacques Lacan, Book IX: Identification,* translated by Cormac Gallagher. London: Karnac (2002).

Lacan, Jacques (1962–1963). *The Seminar of Jacques Lacan, Book X: Anxiety.* Translated by Cormac Gallagher. Eastbourne: Antony Rowe (2001).

Lacan, Jacques (1963–1964). *Seminar of Jacques Lacan, Book XI: The Four Fundamental Concepts of Psychoanalysis,* translated by Alan Sheridan. New York: WW Norton (1992).

Lacan, Jacques (1967). *Écrits,* translated by Bruce Fink. New York: WW Norton (2006).

Lacan, Jacques (1967–1968). *Seminar of Jacques Lacan, Book XV: The Psychoanalytic Act,* translated by Cormac Gallagher. www.lacaninireland.com (2011).

Lacan, Jacques (1969–1970). *Seminar of Jacques Lacan, Book XVII: The Other Side of Psychoanalysis,* translated by Cormac Gallagher. www.lacaninireland.com (2011).

Lacan, Jacques (1972–1973). *The Seminar of Jacques Lacan, Book XX: Encore – On Feminine Sexuality and the Limits of Love and Knowledge,* translated by Bruce Fink. New York: WW Norton (1998).

Lacan, Jacques (1974–1975). The Seminar of Jacques Lacan, Book XXII: R.S.I., Translated by 'Riot Hero'. *Encyclopedia of Psychoanalysis,* https://nosubject.com/File:THE-SEMINAR-OF-JACQUES-LACAN-XXII_RSI.pdf, (2019).

Lacan, Jacques (1975). The Third, translated by Philip Dravers. *The Lacanian Review,* 7:97–108 (2019).

Lacan, Jacques (1975–1976). *The Seminar of Jacques Lacan, Book XXIII: The Sinthome,* translated by A.R. Price. Cambridge, UK: Polity Press (2016).

Laplanche, Jean (1992). *Seduction, Translation and the Drives.* London: Ica Editions.

Laplanche, Jean and Pontalis, Jean-Bernard (1988). *The Language of Psychoanalysis.* New York and London: Routledge.

Laurin, Camille (1964). Sexualité féminine. *Psychanalyse: revue de la société française de psychanalyse,* 7: 15–54.

Le Gaufey, Guy (2019). *Lacan and the Formulae of Sexuation: Exploring Logical Consistency and Clinical Consequences.* London: Routledge.

Levinas, Emanuel (1990) *Difficult Freedom,* translated by S. Hand. Baltimore: Johns Hopkins.

Lévi-Strauss, Claude (1974) *Structural Anthropology,* translated by Claire Jacobson and Brooke Schoepf. New York: Basic Books.

Lodge, David (1984). *Small World: An Academic Romance.* London: Secker & Warburg.

Marx, Carl (1887) *Capital: A Critique of Political Economy, Volume I,* translated by Samuel Moore and Edward Aveling. New York: Humboldt Publishing.

Marx, Carl (1888). Theses on Feuerbach, translated by W. Lough. *Marx/ Engels Selected Works I*, pp. 13–15. Moscow: Progress Publishers (1969).

Miller, Jacque-Alain (1997). Five Lessons on Language and the Real. *Hurly-Burly*, 7: 59–118 (2012).

Mitchell, Juliet & Rose, Jacqueline (1982). *Feminine Sexuality: Jacques Lacan and the École Freudienne*. London: MacMillan Press.

Muller, John (1996). *Beyond the Psychoanalytic Dyad: Developmental Semiotics in Freud, Peirce and Lacan*. London: Routledge.

Parsons, William B. (1999). *The Enigma of the Oceanic Feeling*. Oxford: Oxford University Press.

Peirce, C.S. (1958). *Collected Papers of Charles Sanders Peirce, Vols. 1–6*. Cambridge MA: Harvard University Press.

Perelberg, Rosine Josef (2005). Introduction. *Freud: A Modern Reader*. New York: Routledge

Ragland-Sullivan, Ellie (1992). The Paternal Metaphor: A Lacanian Theory of Language. *Revue Internationale de Philosophie*, 46:49–92.

Roudinesco, Élisabeth (2014). *Lacan: In Spite of Everything*. London: Verso Books.

Sartre, Jean-Paul (1956). *Being and Nothingness: An Essay on Phenomenological Ontology*, translated by Hazel E. Barnes. New York: Random House.

Science Encyclopedia (2022). Jouissance – Lacan in the 1970s: Masculine and Feminine. *Jrank articles*, https://science.jrank.org/pages/ 9860/Jouissance-Lacan-in-1970s-Masculine-Feminine-Jouissances.htm l#ixzz6hdM4n0hp.

Saussure, Ferdinand de (1915). *A Course in General Linguistics*. New York: McGraw-Hill (1959).

Soler, Collette (1995). The Body in the Teaching of Jacques Lacan. *Journal of the Center for Freudian Analysis and Research*, 6:6–38.

Soler, Collette (2014). *Lacan: The Unconscious Reinvented*. London: Routledge.

Stavrakakis, Yannis (1999). *Lacan and the Political*. London: Routledge.

Vanier, Alain (2000). *Lacan: Lacanian Clinical Field*, translated by Susan Fairfield. New York: Other Press.

Verhaeghe, P. (2004). *On Being Normal and Other Disorders: A Manual for Clinical Psychodiagnostics*, translated by S. Jottkandt. New York: Other Press.

Wajcman, Gerard (2003). The Hysteric's Discourse. *The Symptom Online Journal for Lacan*, 4, www.lacan.com/hystericdiscf.htm.

Winnicott, Donald W. (1969). The Use of an Object. *The International Journal of Psychoanalysis*, 50:711–716.

Wittgenstein, Ludwig (1953). *Philosophical Investigations*, translated by G.E.M. Anscombe. London: Macmillan.

Yadlin-Gadot. Shlomit (2016). *Truth Matters: Theory and Practice in Psychoanalysis*. Leiden: Brill Publishers.

Yadlin-Gadot, Shlomit (2021). Lacan on Mind and Body. In Jon Mills (ed.), *Psychoanalysis and the Mind-Body Problem*. London: Routledge.

Žižek, Slavoj (2008). *The Lacanian Real: Television. The Symptom*, 9, fall issue.

Žižek, Slavoj (2016). Can One Exit From the Capitalist Discourse Without Becoming a Saint? *Crisis and Critique*, 3:480–499.

Index

'imaginarized' 72, 107; language and speech 12–14, 36; meaning, and signifiers 13–15; and need 36; and neurosis 56; and Oedipal development 30–33; the Other, the unconscious 15–16; Peircian 7; and political discourse 105, 106–7, 115; relation to the other orders 23–5, 34–5; and sexuation 70–80, 82; and social organization 12–13; the split subject 37–42; in therapy 90–92, 96–102; as triadic 19

therapy 21, 26, 59, 73, 86–7; the analyst as 'playing the fool' 92–3; analyst discourse 104, 110–112, 115; anchoring a new identity 97–102; cut, void, and absence 93–4; from discourse to act 95–6; from knowledge to know-how 96–7; the symptom 87–8; transference 88–92; traversing of the fantasy 95

the 'Thing' ('das Ding') 44, 45, 62; and Oedipal development 30–34; and the Real order 19–20; and signification 8

transference: and the analyst's desire 88–90; and the Imaginary gamut 90–92; love 81

truth: analyst discourse 92, 93–4; *vs.* knowledge 3, 114, 115; and language 62, 81; and political discourse 104–10

unconscious 17, 24; analyst discourse 90, 93–4, 110–111, the 89; aphorisms 118; Freudian 2–3, 117; and the fundamental fantasy 43, 44, 89; jouissance and the Real 97, 98–100; in the neurotic 55–6; in the obsessive 59; Oedipal process 32, 55–6; the Other, and the Symbolic order 15–16; and sexuality 67–8, 80; and the split subject 37–41

Verhaeghe, P. 65

Winnicott, Donald W. 53
Wittgenstein, Ludwig 96

Žižek, Slavoj 62–3

For Product Safety Concerns and Information please contact our EU
representative GPSR@taylorandfrancis.com
Taylor & Francis Verlag GmbH, Kaufingerstraße 24, 80331 München, Germany

www.ingramcontent.com/pod-product-compliance
Lightning Source LLC
Chambersburg PA
CBHW070347270326
41926CB00017B/4022